Catholic Faith Teaching Manual

Level 4 : Pre -Confirmation

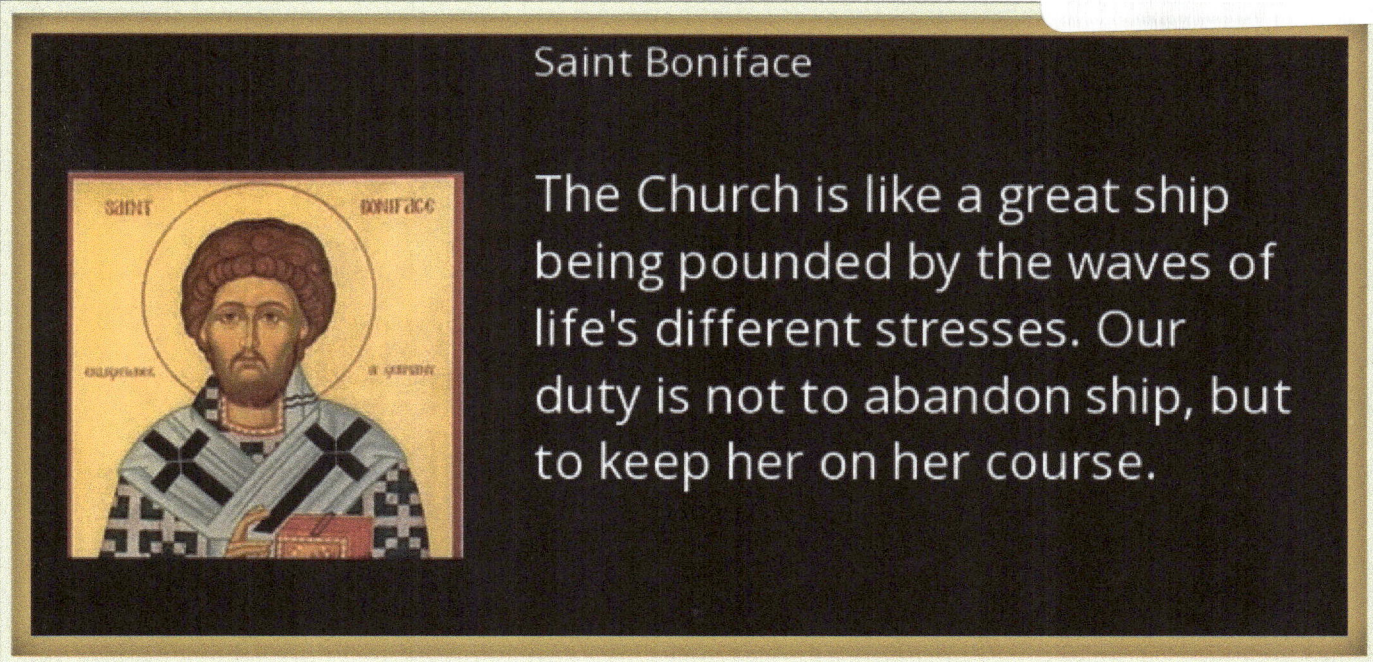

Copyright © 2021 by Father Raymond Taouk. All rights reserved.

"No part of this publication may be reproduced, distributed, or transmitted in any form or by any means, including photocopying, recording, or other electronic or mechanical methods, or by any information storage and retrieval system without the prior written permission of the publisher, except in the case of very brief quotations embodied in critical reviews and certain other noncommercial uses permitted by copyright law."

Co published with JMJ Catholic products.
www.jmjcatholicproducts.com.au
Email : jeanette@jmjcatholicproducts.com.au

ISBN: 9780645021943

TABLE OF CONTENTS

			Page
Lesson 1	Catechism : The First Commandment (Questions 88, 89, 90)		6
	Prayer : The Our Father		7
	Bible Studies : Jesus rides into Jerusalem		8
	The Saints : Saint Denis		11
	Devotions : The Story of Lourdes		12
	General : Fasting		13
Lesson 2	Catechism : The First Commandment (Questions 91, 92, 93)		16
	Prayer : The Our Father continued		17
	Bible Studies : The Last Supper		18
	The Saints : Saint Helen		20
	Devotions : The Story of Lourdes		22
	General : Abstinence		22
Lesson 3	Catechism : Honoring the Saints, Relics, Images (Questions 94, 95, 96)		26
	Prayer : The Our Father (continued)		27
	Bible Studies : The Last supper		28
	The Saints : Saint Genevieve		30
	Devotions : The Story of Lourdes (continued)		32
	General : Feast Days		33
Lesson 4	Catechism : The Second Commandment (Questions 97, 98, 99, 100)		36
	Prayer : The Our Father (continued)		37
	Bible Studies : The Agony in the Garden		38
	The Saints : Saint Brigid of Ireland		40
	Devotions : The Miraculous Medal		42
	General : The ecclesiastical year		43
Lesson 5	Catechism : The Third Commandment (Questions 101, 102, 103, 104, 105)		46
	Prayer : The Hail Mary		47
	Bible Studies : Jesus Before His enemies		48
	The Saints : Saint Giles		50
	Devotions : The Miraculous Medal (continued)		52
	General : The Commandments of the Church		53
Lesson 6	Catechism : The Fourth Commandment (Questions 106, 107, 108)		56
	Prayer : The Hail Mary (continued)		57
	Bible Studies : The Scourging at the Pillar		58
	The Saints : Saint Bernard of Clairvaux		60
	Devotions : The Miraculous Medal (continued)		62
	General : The Four Last Things		63
Lesson 7	Catechism : The Fifth Commandment (Questions 109, 110, 111)		66
	Prayer : The Hail Mary (continued)		67
	Bible Studies : The Crowning with Thorns		68
	The Saints : Saint Joan of Arc		70
	Devotions : The Story of Fatima		72
	General : The Four Marks of the Church		73

Lesson 8	Catechism : The Sixth Commandment (Questions 112, 113, 114)		76
	Prayer : The Hail Mary (continued)		77
	Bible Studies : The Journey to Calvary		78
	The Saints : Saint Jerome Emiliani		80
	Devotions : The Story of Fatima		82
	General : The Seven Steps to the Priesthood		83
Lesson 9	Catechism : The Seventh Commandment (Questions 115, 116, 117, 118)		86
	Prayer : The Morning Offering		87
	Bible Studies : Jesus is nailed to the Cross and dies		88
	The Saints : Saint Thomas More		90
	Devotions : The Story of Fatima		92
	General		93
Lesson 10	Catechism : The Eighth Commandment (Questions 119, 120, 121)		96
	Prayer : The Morning Offering		97
	Bible Studies : Jesus in the Tomb - The Resurrection		98
	The Saints : Saint Boniface		100
	Devotions : The First Saturday's		102
	General : Catholic Etiquette		103
Lesson 11	Catechism : The Ninth and Tenth Commandment (Questions 122, 123, 124, 125, 126)		106
	Prayer : The Act of Contrition		107
	Bible Studies : Jesus Appears to His Friends		108
	The Saints : Saint Peter Canisius		110
	Devotions : Fatima - The Last Vision		112
	General : Catholic Etiquette		113
Lesson 12	Catechism : The First Commandment of the Church (Questions 127, 128, 129)		116
	Prayer : The Act of Contrition (continued)		117
	Bible Studies : Jesus Promises the Holy Ghost		118
	The Saints : Saint Germain		119
	Devotions : Sacred Heart of Jesus - The Nine First Friday's		122
	General : Catholic Etiquette		123
Lesson 13	Catechism : The Second Commandment of the Church (Questions 130, 131, 132)		126
	Prayer : The Act of Contrition (continued)		127
	Bible Studies : The Ascension		128
	The Saints : Saint Cuthbert		129
	Devotions : Sacred Heart of Jesus - The Nine First Friday's		132
	General : Catholic Etiquette		133
Lesson 14	Catechism : The Third, Fourth, Fifth and Sixth Commandment of the Church (Questions 133, 134, 135, 136)		136
	Prayer : A definition of Prayer		137
	Bible Studies : The Coming of the Holy Spirit		138
	The Saints : Saint Wenceslaus		140
	Devotions : Sacred Heart of Jesus - The Nine First Friday's		142
	General : Catholic Etiquette		143
Lesson 15	Catechism Questions 88 to 186		146

Lesson 1

Level 4

Pre - Confirmation

Catechism

Each lesson we are going to study some catechism questions. This is the most important part of your lesson. These questions you must learn by heart so that you will come to know a great deal about God and His wonderful creation. Level Three studied forty two catechism questions, so we commence this Level with Catechism Question 88. May God bless you in your study of Himself and His holy Church.

In Level Four Catechism, we are going to study the Ten Commandments and the Commandments of the Church. These are very important to us as the Commandments are the first and most obvious way we know that we are doing the will of God.

During Our Lord's life a man asked Him what he must do to be saved and the first answer given was to follow the Commandments. Thus, we will study them this level as our catechism topic.

The First Commandment

88. **What is the first commandment of God?**

    The first commandment of God is:
    I am the Lord thy God; thou shalt not have strange gods before Me.

89. **What are we commanded by the first commandment?**

    By the first commandment we are commanded to offer to God alone the supreme worship that is due Him.

90. **How do we worship God?**

    We worship God by acts of faith, hope, and charity, and by adoring Him and praying to Him.

We remember from Level Three that the first three Commandments deal with our relationship with God, whereas the last seven Commandments deal with our relationship with our neighbour.
Each Commandment commands something and forbids something.
The spirit of the First Commandment is that we offer to God alone the supreme worship that is due to Him. Anything going against that is a breaking of this Commandment.

Question 1   ◆   What are we commanded by the first commandment?
Question 2   ◆   How do we worship God?

Level 4 - Lesson 1

Prayer

In previous levels, each lesson we have learned a different prayer. By now, we should have a good number of prayers that we know by heart. Many we say every day, and others from time to time.

In this level we are not going to learn any new prayers, but we are going to study the words (meanings) of some of the more common and popular prayers. It is very important to know what we are saying when praying!

The Our Father (The Lord's Prayer)

Our Father, Who art in heaven:

This prayer which Our Lord Himself taught us, is addressed to God the Father. When we say these words, we are demonstrating our faith by saying that God is in heaven; we are showing our faith in God, but also in the existence of heaven.

Hallowed be Thy name:

We have used this word "hallowed" all our lives; but do we know what it means? It means that we are calling the name of God, holy. In the Old Testament, the Jews revered God's holy name so much, they would never even say it.

Question 3 ◆ When we pray the Our Father, to Whom do we speak?

Question 4 ◆ What do we mean by Hallowed be Thy name?

Question 5 ◆ Who taught us the prayer, The Our Father?

Bible Story

In this Level we will be looking at stories from the New Testament only. In fact, we will be studying only a very brief period in Our Lord's life; from His triumphal entry into Jerusalem on Palm Sunday, to the Descent of the Holy Ghost on Pentecost Sunday. Therefore a great deal of our studies this level will be on the Passion and Death of Our Saviour.

Jesus Rides Into Jerusalem

A short time after Lazarus had come to life again, Jesus took supper with Lazarus, and Mary, and Martha, and the next day He said to His disciples: "It is time we went to Jerusalem." When they had come to Mount Olivet, Jesus told two of His disciples to go to the next village, and that they would there find, tied to a gate, a donkey with its young one, called a colt. No man had ridden yet on this colt. Jesus told them: "When you find this colt, the man you see minding it will ask you what you want, and you are to say you want the colt, for the Lord is in need of it, and then he will let you take it."

And the disciples going, did as Jesus told them. When they brought the colt to Jesus, it had no harness or saddle on it, so they spread their clothes over its back, and made Jesus sit on it. A very great crowd of people now came, and they cut down boughs of trees, carried palm branches in their hands, and strewed their clothes and boughs along the way, for Jesus to ride over.

They shouted and said "Blessed is He that cometh in the name of the Lord." and so they entered Jerusalem in great joy. The whole city came out to meet Him, and they said: "Who is this?" and the people said: "This is Jesus."

Jesus went to the Temple, and crowds came with Him, and they brought to Him the blind, and deaf, and lame, and dumb, and all sick persons, and Jesus cured them, so that they were all glad and filled with joy, even the little children called out: "Hosanna to the Son of David; blessed be the Son of David."

The Jewish priests and learned men, hearing the children, were angry, and they asked Jesus if He heard what the children said. Jesus always loved little children, and must have liked their song best of all, for He said: "Yes, I hear. Out of the mouths of infants and of sucklings thou hast perfected praise."

Question 6 ◆ Why did the people cut down palms when Jesus entered
Question 7 ◆ What did the people shout out as Jesus entered Jerusalem?
Question 8 ◆ What did Jesus ask the Apostles to get for Him?

Level 4 - Lesson 1

The Saints

Saint Denis

There were Christians in France very soon after the death and resurrection of Jesus. The country, which was then called Gaul, was part of the Roman Empire, so things that were done at Rome soon left their mark there also; and when one of the Emperors, Valerian, ordered a great persecution of the Christians, those in Gaul suffered as much as those in Rome. Almost all of them were killed, and after the terror was over the Pope decided he must send some missionaries to preach the Gospel and to encourage those Christians that were left.

The man he chose, who was known to be very brave and good and was very learned in the Christian Faith, was named Denis. Denis took with him his two great friends Rusticus, a priest, and Eleutherius, a deacon; and with some others they traveled the roads of Gaul until they came to an island in the middle of a great river – the island in the river Seine which is now part of Paris. Here they settled and built a church where they began to practice their religion and to preach.

They made so many converts that the pagan priests became very angry and asked the Governor Sisinnius to put a stop by force to the new teaching. Sisinnius sent for Denis and his companions, and ordered them to sacrifice to the pagan gods. When they refused to do this they were put in prison and tortured, but they still said that Jesus was truly God and that it was their duty to tell as many people as they could about His resurrection. So they were taken to a high hill overlooking the city and there they were beheaded. That Paris hill is still called Montmartre, which means "the Mount of the Martyrs."

The bodies of Denis and his companions were thrown into the river Seine so that they might float away and be altogether forgotten; but a Christian lady named Catulla rescued them and gave them a proper burial, marking their graves with a little shrine.

Years later, when Christianity became the religion of the Roman Empire, a great church was built there so that all Frenchmen might remember Denis, the first Bishop of Paris and "the Apostle of France." Here most of the kings of France were buried. Over the altar the king's standard always hung when he himself was not in battle. And when there were battles to be fought the war-cry of the soldiers was "Saint Denis for France," for he became the patron saint of France as Saint George is the patron saint of England. His Feast day is on October 9.

Question 9 ◆ Which Roman Emperor ordered a great persecution of the Christians at the time of Saint Denis?

Question 10 ◆ Where was Saint Denis killed?

Question 11 ◆ What does Montmatre mean?

Question 12 ◆ Who is the Patron Saint of France?

Devotions

Throughout the history of the Church, Our Blessed Lord and His holy Mother have, from time to time appeared to certain souls to give them messages, either for the individuals concerned or for the whole world. The Church examines these events carefully and then pronounces judgment as to whether the faithful can follow these apparitions or not. In addition to the true apparitions, there have been many false ones, inspired by the devil, so it is very important to listen to what the Church has to say.

When heaven speaks to us through these apparitions, it is always with good reason. Our Lord or Our Lady have something to tell us that is an important help in our salvation. In this Level, we are going to study a number of these apparitions, many of which have taken place in the past two hundred years. Our first topic for discussion is the Story of Lourdes.

The Story of Lourdes

To understand the story of Lourdes, it is necessary to understand the story of the seer, (the person to whom Our Lady appeared), Saint Bernadette. Bernadette Soubirous was born in 1844 and was the oldest of the four surviving children of the nine born to her mother (five had died as babies). When Saint Bernadette was about twelve, her father lost his job and the family had to move to a house with only one room. It was just big enough for three beds and a fire place to cook the meals and to keep them warm during winter. Their neighbour in the same building were their cousin's livestock (animals). The walls were made of stone and the room was always damp which did not help Saint Bernadette's asthma.

On February 11, 1858, the fourteen year old Bernadette and two friends went to gather firewood. They stopped near the Gave River to remove their shoes and wade across the small stream near a natural grotto at a place called Massabielle. The other two children raced ahead, but Bernadette, being afraid the icy water would bring on an asthma attack, hesitated. Suddenly, she heard the sound of a rushing wind and saw a bright light near the grotto. In this light appeared a lady, so beautiful that to see her again one would be willing to die. Saint Bernadette started praying the Rosary. The lady smiled and joined in at the Glory Be prayers. The lady asked Saint Bernadette to return fifteen times, which she promised to do.

During the apparitions, the lady gave Saint Bernadette a number of messages. The main purpose of most of her requests was to ask people to do penance for their sins. The lady gave Saint Bernadette some messages for herself which she never revealed. She also asked for a chapel to be built at the grotto, and for processions.

Question 13 ♦ In what year did Our Lady appear to Saint Bernadette?
Question 14 ♦ What two things in particular did Our Lady ask for?
Question 15 ♦ What was the main purpose of Our Lady's requests?

Fasting

Fasting

From the earliest times the Church has taught its children to fast. It has followed the example of our Divine Saviour Who spent forty days in the desert fasting, before beginning His public life. Jesus often spoke of the necessity of fasting. There are two main types of fasting in the Church; the fast before Holy Communion and the days of fast. Let us look at each of these separately.

Fasting before Holy Communion:

The Church prescribes that anyone who wishes to receive Our Lord in Holy Communion, fast for one hour before receiving the Sacred Host. This means that for a period of one hour, no food or liquid (except water) may be taken. It was not so many years ago that the fast was three hours before Holy Communion. In fact, your grandparents will probably remember when the fast was from midnight!

Under pain of sin we must keep the one hour fast, but when possible, we should try to fast for a longer period, perhaps three hours.

Days of Fast:

A fast day is one on which only one full meal is allowed but two other small meals may be taken (these two meals combined, must be less than the quantity of the larger meal).

No food can be eaten between meals, but one may drink water, lemonade, tea/coffee and other non-nourishing drinks.

Everyone aged between 18 years and 59 years are bound under mortal sin to fast on Ash Wednesday and Good Friday. (In earlier days, it was obligatory to fast during all of Lent).
The Church encourages, however, that we fast during Lent, on certain Vigils and on Ember days. Fasting is also highly recommended when we are asking God for something. Prayer and fasting go together very well.

Question 16 ◆ Who are bound to fast?

Question 17 ◆ On which days are we bound to fast?

Question 18 ◆ How long is the fast before Holy Communion?

Lesson 2

Level 4

Pre - Confirmation

Catechism

The First Commandment

91. How does a Catholic sin against faith?

A Catholic sins against faith by not believing what God has revealed, and by taking part in non-Catholic worship.

92. What are the sins against hope?

The sins against hope are presumption and despair.

93. What are the chief sins against charity?

The chief sins against charity are hatred of God and of our neighbour, envy, sloth, and scandal.

By now (level four), it is most necessary to study your catechism questions in some detail. As you get older, it is not sufficient to just learn your catechism questions by heart, (although it is very important) but to understand the questions and answers as best you can. Whether you are learning catechism at school, at home or after Mass on Sunday, strive to do your best and ensure that you understand what is being taught.

The above questions are a study of the sins against the three theological virtues of faith, hope and charity. Therefore, these are the things we must avoid.

Let us look in particular at the sins against hope, presumption and despair.

Presumption means that we think it is alright to live a wicked or sinful life, while at the same time thinking we will be saved because Jesus died for us.

Despair is the opposite. It means that we believe that we are so wicked that not even God can help us; it can lead to suicide (the killing of oneself).

Question 1	♦	What are the chief sins against charity?
Question 2	♦	Give a short definition of presumption.
Question 3	♦	What are we commanded by the first commandment?

Level 4 - Lesson 2

Prayer

The Our Father (The Lord's Prayer) continued...

Thy Kingdom come

When we pray the words, Thy Kingdom come, we are begging God that His heavenly kingdom be also here on this earth. That is, that the world in which we live, be a true reflection of heaven. We are asking that Christ's Church here on Earth, be loved and followed in all places during our lives, not only after our deaths.

Thy Will be done on Earth, as it is in Heaven

This line of the Our Father is almost an explanation of the previous line. For God's kingdom to be on this Earth, His Will needs to be followed by us as it is followed by the angels and saints in Heaven. Thus, we are asking Our Father in Heaven to give us the graces necessary to do His holy Will in our lives that we may one day do His holy Will for all eternity.

Question 4 ◆ In what line of the Our Father are we asking that His heavenly Kingdom be also here on this Earth?
Question 5 ◆ What is meant by, Thy Will be done on Earth as it is in Heaven?
Question 6 ◆ What is another name for the Our Father?

Bible Story

The Last Supper – Part One

You remember that the Jews had some laws given them by God which they kept in great state. One was how to celebrate the great feast of the Pasch, when they killed a lamb and ate a special kind of bread. When the time came, Jesus told Peter and John to go to the city and prepare a room for this feast. Jesus told them that in the city they would meet a man carrying a pitcher of water on his head and that they were to follow this man into any house he entered; that they were to ask the owner of that house where was the room for Jesus and His disciples to eat the lamb, and he would show them a furnished room, all ready. In the evening Jesus came to this place with His twelve disciples, and sat down with them at the table, and ate what is called the "Lord's Last Supper."

The Washing of the Feet.

At the Last Supper Jesus got up from the table, and tied a towel round Himself, and taking a basin of water, washed the feet of His disciples, and dried them with the towel. When Jesus came to Peter to wash his feet, Peter did not like to let Our Lord do such a humble act, and said: "Lord, are you to wash my feet?" and Jesus said, "Yes." But Peter said to Him: "No, you shall never wash my feet." And Jesus answered him: "If I do not wash your feet, then you shall have no part with Me." Rather than this should be the case, Peter said: "Lord, not only my feet, but also my hands and my head."

Jesus then told His disciples why He washed their feet. He said: "You call Me Master and Lord: and you say well, for so I am. If then I, being your Lord and Master, have washed your feet, you also ought to wash one another's feet. For I have given you an example, that as I have done to you, so you do also." This was to teach His disciples, and us also, to be humble and clean (good) of heart. Jesus knew, even while He was speaking, that there was one of His disciples there who was not clean (good) of heart, and his name was Judas.

Question 7 ◆ Explain how Jesus and His disciples came to find the room in which they ate the Last Supper.

Question 8 ◆ What did Jesus teach the Apostles by the washing of the feet?

Question 9 ◆ What did the people shout out as Jesus entered Jerusalem?

The Saints

Saint Helen

When the Emperor Constantius died at York in the year 306AD, the Roman Army immediately proclaimed his son Constantine, who was in Britain with his father, Emperor in his place. The new Emperor's mother was Helen, who, some people have said, was the daughter of Old King Cole, the Prince of Colchester, though others think that she was the daughter of an innkeeper there. Whichever it was, Colchester is very proud of her, and there is still a statue of her on the Town Hall. But the things she did which made her a saint happened long after she had left Britain with her son Constantine and gone back to Rome, and in the city which was named after him Constantinople.

Helen, like most of the people who lived in Britain at that time, was a pagan, and her son, like her, believed in the old gods and goddesses of the Romans. But Christianity was getting stronger and stronger, and Constantine had heard about Jesus and the Cross.

Though Constantine had been proclaimed Emperor by the soldiers at York, there were many powerful people in other parts of the Empire and in Rome itself who would not acknowledge him, and he had to fight hard and for a long time to get the throne. Just before the battle which would decide everything, he had a dream or a vision of a flaming Cross in the sky, and the words "By this sign shalt thou conquer." So he made a vow that, if he won the battle, he would make his whole Empire Christian. He kept his word, and after he had become Emperor made a law by which Christianity became the religion everywhere the Romans ruled.

Of course, his mother Helen was one of the first to be baptised, and as she learnt about the Cross where Jesus died she began to wonder what had happened to that particular Cross on Mount Calvary. The more she thought about it the more she felt that she ought to go to Jerusalem and try to find it.

At last, though she was nearly eighty years old, Constantine made arrangements for her to travel to Jerusalem, and told every one there to give her all the help they could. No one thought that she would be able to find the True Cross, for by that time it was nearly three hundred years since Jesus had been crucified. But Helen, in her heart, was quite sure that God meant her to find it.

It had happened that one of the earlier Roman Emperors, Hadrian, who hated Christians, had built over Calvary and the Holy Sepulchre a terrace, three hundred feet long on which was a statue of the Roman god Jupiter and a temple to the goddess Venus. This had been done less than a hundred years after the Crucifixion, so Helen thought that, if she had this terrace destroyed and got down to the foundations, she might find things as they used to be. But even when the workmen had done as she told them, there was an enormous amount of digging to be done, and no real certainty of finding anything.

At last, however, they started to search in a place which Helen had dreamt about, near a little rock cistern, and there they unearthed three crosses. They all looked very much the same, and there seemed no way to tell which of them was the Cross on which Jesus suffered. But Helen found a very sick man, who was nearly dying, and prayed to God that, if he was laid on the True Cross, he might be cured.

The Saints

So they took him up and laid him very gently on the first cross. Nothing happened. Then they laid him on the second, and still nothing happened. But when his body touched the third he was immediately cured. So all knew that was the True Cross, and Helen ordered the builders to build a great church in which it could be kept. A piece of wood she took back with her reverently to Rome, as well as two of the nails which had been found near it; and when she got home she built there another church called "The Holy Cross in Jerusalem," where the wood and the nails were kept in a shrine.

For hundreds of years pilgrims went from all over Europe to Jerusalem to see the True Cross, until it was destroyed by enemies of Christianity who captured the Holy City; but every year on May 3 the Church still keeps the feast of the Finding of the Cross by Saint Helen. Her Feast Day is August 18.

Question 10 ◆ Who found the true Cross?
Question 11 ◆ Who was Saint Helen's son?
Question 12 ◆ Where was Saint Denis killed?

Devotions

The Story of Lourdes
(Part Two)

During one of the apparitions, Our Lady asked Saint Bernadette to drink from the spring; not knowing of a spring, she turned and began walking toward the Gave River, but the lady called her back. She indicated a spot on the ground, and Saint Bernadette immediately dug into the earth. The people watching were astounded to see the little visionary apparently eating mud. From this spot, an underground spring welled up which today provides miraculous water for the pilgrims to Lourdes.

On one occasion, Our Lady said to Saint Bernadette, "I do not promise you happiness in this world, but in the next". It was very prophetic, as Saint Bernadette suffered much during her life, but is now one of the elect in heaven.

Saint Bernadette was investigated by the police and by the local religious authorities. She never wavered in her story, and she insisted that the lady had asked for a chapel. The parish priest told Saint Bernadette to ask the lady her name; at the final apparition, the lady folded her hands and said, "I am the Immaculate Conception".

Saint Bernadette did not understand the words, and had to keep repeating them to herself as she went to tell the priest. She asked him what the words meant, in spite of the fact that Pius IX had proclaimed the dogma of the Immaculate Conception just four years previously, in 1854.

Question 13   ◆   What did Our Lady say to Saint Bernadette concerning suffering?
Question 14   ◆   When Saint Bernadette asked the lady her name, what was the reply?
Question 15   ◆   In what year did Our Lady appear to Saint Bernadette?

General

Abstinence

"Whatsoever you bind on earth, it shall be bound in heaven…" These words of our dear Lord gave power to the Church to make laws that bind Catholics under pain of sin. One such law is the law of abstinence.

What is a day of abstinence? A day of abstinence is a day on which we are not allowed to eat meat. Who are obliged to observe the days of abstinence? All baptised persons fourteen years of age and over are obliged to observe the abstinence days of the church unless they are excused or dispensed. Why does the Church command us to abstain? The Church commands us to abstain in order that we may control the desires of the flesh, raise our minds more freely to God and make satisfaction for sin.

When are we commanded to abstain? We are commanded to abstain on Ash Wednesday and on all Fridays unless a holy day of obligation falls on a Friday.

Question 16 ◆ What do we mean by abstinence?
Question 17 ◆ Who is bound to abstain?
Question 18 ◆ How long is the fast before Holy Communion?

Lesson 3

Level 4

Pre - Confirmation

Catechism

Honouring the Saints, Relics and Images

94. **Does the first commandment forbid us to honour the saints in heaven?**

    The first commandment does not forbid us to honour the saints in heaven, as long as we do not give them the honour that belongs to God alone.

95. **When we pray to the saints what do we ask them to do?**

    When we pray to the saints we ask them to offer their prayers to God for us.

96. **Do we pray to the crucifix or to the images of Christ and of the saints?**

    We do not pray to the crucifix or to the images of Christ and of the saints, but to the persons of whom they remind us.

There is much confusion among non-Catholics, and even among Catholics as to the honouring of the Saints and sacred images. We must understand well what the first commandment permits and forbids. Non-Catholics say is it wrong to carry a picture of Our Lady in our wallet or to hang a picture of a saint on the wall. They do not understand what we do when we hold these images. The images are a representation of the person we honour; we do not honour the image itself. Most Catholic fathers carry a photograph of their wives and/or children in their wallets. They look at the photograph and are reminded of the actual people. It is the same when we kneel before a statue of Our Lady. We are not praying to the statue (like the pagans do), but to Our Blessed Mother herself who is represented by the statue.

Question 1	♦	Does the first commandment forbid us to honour the saints in heaven?
Question 2	♦	Do we pray to the crucifix or to the images of Christ and of the saints?
Question 3	♦	How does a Catholic sin against faith?

Level 4 - Lesson 3

Prayer

The Our Father (The Lord's Prayer) continued…

Give us this day our daily bread

The second half of the Our Father is principally a prayer of petition; we are asking God the Father to help us in our needs. The first things we ask for are our material needs; our food in particular, but more generally, all that we need for our bodies.

And forgive us our trespasses as we forgive those who trespass against us

How many times have we prayed the Our Father, and not understood this line? Oh, how very important it is. We are asking here for Our Father to judge us as we judge others; forgive us our sins Lord, as we forgive those who sin against us. So, when we pray the Our Father, remember, we are asking God to judge us as we judge our neighbour. Perhaps we had better think more charitably when judging our neighbour if we want a more lenient judgment from God.

Forgive us our trespasses

Question 4	◆	What type of prayer is the second half of the Our Father?
Question 5	◆	What are we asking of God the Father when we say, And forgive us our trespasses as we forgive those who trespass against us?
Question 6	◆	In what line of the Our Father are we asking that His heavenly Kingdom be also here on this Earth?

Bible Story

The Last Supper – Part Two

After Jesus had washed His disciples' feet, and whilst they were eating, He said: "Amen I say to you, that one of you is about to betray Me." The disciples were sorry to hear this, and each said: "Is it I Lord?" And Judas, that did betray Him, said: "Is it I, Rabbi?" (Master). He saith to him: "Thou hast said it." And whilst they were at Supper, Jesus took bread, and blessed and broke, and gave to His disciples, and said:

"Take ye and eat, this is My Body." And taking the chalice, He gave thanks, and gave to them, saying: **"Drink ye all of this, for this is My Blood."** This was the greatest, kindest, and most loving act that even God could do. Jesus could do no more than this.

Never forget these words of Jesus: **"This is My Body,"** and **"This is My Blood."** Jesus, then, at this feast, changed the bread into His Body, and the wine into His Blood.

No one can understand this fully. When you go to Church, and bend your knee at the altar, you do so because you are told "The Blessed Sacrament" is there. You know now, how It came there.

The Blessed Sacrament is Jesus. Jesus gave us Himself at that Last Supper; and although we cannot see Him as He was then, as a man speaking to His disciples, yet the Blessed Sacrament is Jesus, and He is there on our altar, hidden in that "White Host," the very same good, kind, loving Jesus who was speaking to His disciples at the Last Supper. We ought to go often to our churches, to see Jesus, and talk to Him; to ask Him for everything we want; no little thing is too small, and no big thing is too great to ask Jesus.

Question 7	♦	What great gift did Jesus give us at the Last Supper?
Question 8	♦	Who did Our Lord say would betray Him?
Question 9	♦	Who is present in our churches?
Question 10	♦	What did Jesus teach the Apostles by the washing of the feet?

The Saints

Saint Genevieve

When Saint Germain was on his way to Britain he stopped at a little village called Nanterre, about eight miles from Paris. All the people round about came to see the famous man, the Duke who had become a bishop, and when a great crowd had gathered he preached to them. While he was speaking he noticed particularly a little girl who, though she was only seven, was listening very carefully. When he had finished he asked her to come and talk to him. Her name, she told him, was Genevieve; she lived in the village with her parents; and, though she was very young, she had quite made up her mind to spend her life serving Jesus Christ. The Bishop gave her a little medal with a cross engraved on it.

"Wear it always," he said, "to remind you that you have promised your life to Jesus; and be content with it instead of gold brooches and jewels that you might wear."

When Genevieve was fifteen her parents died and she went to live with her godmother in Paris. Here she led the life of a nun, spending her time in prayer and in doing good to people and, as she grew older, in helping other girls and women who were trying to live the same kind of life.

In her prayers God sometimes allowed Genevieve to see things which were going to happen, but when she warned people about the future they laughed at her and took no notice. Some people even said that she was not really good at all, but was only trying to make a name for herself by pretending to say long prayers and to see visions. Once they got so angry that they even tried to drown her.

Then in the year 451AD, when Genevieve was about thirty, the people of Paris realised that one of the things she had told them about was really happening. The barbarians were sweeping over Gaul (France). The last and worst invasion had come. From the east the Huns, led by Attila, the "Scourge of God," had reached Gaul, killing, burning, and plundering through all the land. Attila was different from the other barbarian leaders who had begun to attack the countries of the Roman Empire as soon as the Roman army was too weak to defend them. The others had wished to conquer and to rule. The Huns and their leader only wanted to kill and destroy, just for the love of death and destruction; and all men knew they would show no mercy.

The citizens of Paris decided that their only chance of safety was to leave their city and to flee as fast and as far as they could. They were getting ready to do this when Genevieve spoke to them. She told them that they were wrong, and that if they really trusted in God and prayed to Him, if they really repented of their sins and showed they were in earnest by doing penance for them, they would be spared. Some of the people were still in favour of flight, but others remembered that in the past Genevieve had told them the truth even if they had not believed her – and gradually the city became calm again. The citizens would do as she said – and wait.

And then, by what seemed a miracle, Attila changed his course. Instead of taking the road to Paris, he suddenly altered his direction and turned off towards Orleans, leaving the capital untouched.

Saint Genevieve's Feast day is January 3rd.

The Saints

Level 4 - Lesson 3

Question 11	◆	In what country did Saint Genevieve live?
Question 12	◆	What did Saint Genevieve tell the people of Paris to do for the city to be saved from Attila?
Question 13	◆	What did Saint Helen find?

Devotions

The Story of Lourdes
(Part Three)

After the final apparition, eight more years past for Saint Bernadette at Lourdes. When she was sixteen, the local priest arranged for her to live with the nuns because of her poor health. Later, he suggested to Saint Bernadette that she might like to become a nun, but she answered, "It is impossible, Monsignor. You know very well that I am poor. I haven't got the necessary dowry." Divine Providence overcame this difficulty. In July 1866 Saint Bernadette left Lourdes to join the Congregation of the Sisters of Charity of Nevers. Her name as a religious was Sister Marie Bernarde.

SAINTE BERNADETTE SOUBIROUS

From the time of the apparitions and even whilst still a sister at the convent, Saint Bernadette was questioned numerous times about the apparitions of Our Lady. She bore this constant questioning with great patience. Saint Bernadette was deeply devoted to the Blessed Mother for the rest of her life. When one of the sisters brought up the topic of the apparitions, Saint Bernadette calmly asked her what she did with a broom when she was finished with it. She continued, "You put it behind a door, and that is what the Virgin has done with me. While I was useful, She used me, and now She has put me behind the door".

Saint Bernadette died on April 16th 1879. Her body never corrupted and is now resting peacefully in the Convent of Nevers.

Lourdes is today a place of pilgrimage for thousands of souls who implore Our Lady for bodily and spiritual help. Our Lady asked for a chapel to be built at the site of the apparitions; today, a basilica stands there as a witness to the wonderful events which took place in 1858.

Our Lady's message for us all in this sad, anti-Catholic world is to do penance for our sins and the sins of the world. Let us be devoted also to our heavenly Mother under the title of the Immaculate Conception, whose feast we celebrate on December 8th.

Question 14	♦	Why do people go to Lourdes today?
Question 15	♦	When is the feast of the Immaculate Conception?
Question 16	♦	What special privilege did God grant to the body of Saint Bernadette after her death?
Question 17	♦	When Saint Bernadette asked the lady her name, what was the reply?

Level 4 - Lesson 3

General

Feast Days

The Church has set up a liturgical calendar whereby certain days are celebrated as feasts, other days are days of penance and so on. In this lesson we are going to look at Feast Days in the Church calendar. What they are and the divisions between different types of feast.

Feast days are celebrated in honour of God, His holy Mother Mary, the angels and the saints. On a feast day, the Proper of the Mass (Gospel, Epistle etc.) is dedicated to the person whose feast it is. You will have noticed while studying the Saints' section of your lessons, that we give the feast day for that saint.

The feasts are divided into four main groups; First Class, Second Class, Third Class and Commemorations. As a general rule, feasts of Our Lord are Feasts of the First Class (the highest ranking), although some are of the Second Class. Feast of Our Lady are principally of the Second Class, but a number are of the First Class (e.g. The Immaculate Conception). Most Saints feast days are of the Third Class, but they can be of the First or Second Class (e.g. most of the Apostles are of the Second Class).

Added to this, certain places celebrate a First Class Feast which would normally only be a Commemoration of a Second or Third Class Feast, e.g. Australia has as its principal Patron, Mary Help of Christians; thus a First Class Feast; in the rest of the world is only a Commemoration.

A School which has a certain patron saint, would celebrate that feast as a First Class Feast, although elsewhere it may only be a Second or Third Class Feast.

The details above are only a guide and are not meant to confuse you, but to show how everything in God's Church is ordered, even to the listing of Feast days. God set order in the world and He wants us to be ordered in our work, ordered in our recreation and ordered in our prayer life.

Marian Calender

1st Jan - Solemnity of Mary, Mother of God
2nd Feb - The Purification of the Blessed Virgin Mary
25th Mar - the Annunciation of the Lord
31st May - The Visitation of the Blessed Virgin Mary
15th Aug - Assumption of the Blessed Virgin Mary
8th Sep - The Nativity of the Blessed Virgin Mary
11th Oct - The Queenship of Mary
21st Nov - The Presentation of the Blessed Virgin Mary
8th Dec - The Immaculate Conception

Question 18 ◆ What are the four divisions of Feast Days?
Question 19 ◆ What Class Feast are most feasts of Our Lord?
Question 20 ◆ What do we mean by abstinence?

Lesson 4

Level 4

Pre - Confirmation

Catechism

The Second Commandment

97. What is the second commandment of God?

The second commandment of God is: Thou shalt not take the name of the Lord thy God in vain.

98. What are we commanded by the second commandment?

By the second commandment we are commanded always to speak with reverence of God, of the saints, and of holy things.

99. What is meant by taking God's name in vain?

By taking God's name in vain is meant that the name of God or the holy name of Jesus Christ is used without reverence.

100. What is cursing?

Cursing is the calling down of some evil on a person, place, or thing.

God's holy Name is sacred. We use it when we pray, we use it when we teach others, we use it when we hold good, Catholic conversation, but we should never use it unnecessarily.
We should never use it in times of anger. Nor should we make jokes about God's Name.
It is a holy Name that demands respect at all times.
If we hear someone else misuse Our Lord's Name, quietly say a little aspiration like, My Jesus Mercy or Blessed be the Name of God or some other.

Question 1	◆	What are we commanded by the second commandment?
Question 2	◆	What is meant by taking God's name in vain?
Question 3	◆	When we pray to the saints what do we ask them to do?

Level 4 - Lesson 4

Prayer

The Our Father (The Lord's Prayer) continued…

And lead us not into temptation

Of course Our Lord does not tempt us, but He allows the world, the flesh and the devil to tempt us. He does this to test us that we may be purified on this Earth and thus escape Hell and even Purgatory. When we say these words in the Our Father, we are asking God to give us all the graces we need to overcome these temptations, that we might prove our love for Him. We do not want to be like Pharaoh, whose heart was hardened when Moses asked him to let the people go. Pharaoh so hated God that God withdrew His graces from Pharaoh and Pharaoh was unable to resist the temptation. When saying these words, we are asking God to protect us from these strong temptations which are ever before us.

But deliver us from evil. Amen

Our final petition in this great prayer is that God so showers us with grace, that the devil and all evil will be kept from us. We are asking God, that even if we have fallen into sin, He will rescue us through the Sacrament of Penance. The word Amen means 'So be it' or I agree.

This prayer we pray so many times each day is so rich in meaning and grace. Let us resolve to say it more reverently and fervently always and have great confidence in our Heavenly Father Who created us, keeps us in existence and to Whom this prayer is addressed.

Question 4 ◆ What are we asking of God when we pray the words, And lead us not into temptation?

Question 5 ◆ What is meant by the word Amen?

Question 6 ◆ What are we asking of God the Father when we say, And forgive us our trespasses as we forgive those who trespass against us?

Bible Story

The Agony in the Garden

Jesus now went to a garden called Gethsemane with His disciples. He was very sad, and He told them not to follow Him, but to stay where they were for a little, as He wished to pray alone. Jesus then went by Himself and prayed, saying: "My Father, if it be possible, let this chalice pass from Me. Nevertheless, not as I will, but as Thou wilt." Jesus then went back to the three disciples nearest Him, but He found them all asleep, and He said to Peter: "What! Could you not watch one hour with Me. Watch ye and pray that ye enter not into temptation. The spirit, indeed, is willing, but the flesh is weak." Three times Jesus went and prayed and used the same words, and each time found the disciples on His return fast asleep.

Jesus was in such sorrow and trouble in these prayers that He was bathed in agony with sweat, which became as drops of blood trickling down to the ground. He saw all the sins of the world then, yours and mine, and He saw, too, that many, even after He had died for them, would not love Him, but would sin and grieve Him to the very end. He taught us in this agony of prayer how we ought to pray to God to be spared a trial, but at the same time to say, no matter how much it hurts us, "God's will be done." After these prayers, Jesus went again to the disciples and awoke them, and said: "Rise; let us go; behold, he is at hand that will betray Me."

When they had gone a little way, they met a great crowd of people and soldiers, and Judas was with them. Judas had told the soldiers that the man he would kiss would be Jesus and to take that man. So Judas went up to Jesus, and said; "Hail, Master," and kissed Him, and Jesus said to him: "Judas dost thou betray the Son of Man with a kiss?" The soldiers then went to take Jesus, but Peter took out his sword and cut off the ear of one of them. Jesus told him to put away his sword, and touching the man's ear, He healed it, and gave Himself up quietly to the soldiers. When the disciples saw that Jesus was taken they ran away; Peter and John followed at a distance.

Question 7 ♦ When Jesus went and prayed, what did His Apostles do?
Question 8 ♦ How many times did Jesus go and pray?
Question 9 ♦ Who betrayed Jesus?

The Saints

Saint Brigid of Ireland

About the same time as Saint Genevieve was living in France there was in Ireland another great woman who was to become a saint. Her name was Brigid. Her father was a chieftain and her mother a slave in his household with whom he had fallen in love. Many wonderful stories are told of Brigid's childhood - how wild birds would become tame and let her stroke them, and how the linnet would sing its first song for her.

Men said of her: "She dips her fingers in the stream and the ice melts. She breathes upon the world and the winter is gone." There was a tale that when she worked in the dairy she would only half fill a jar with butter, saying: "God will add something to it," and each jar would became miraculously full. And when she was looking after sheep in the fields she would pray by a flat white stone which she called her altar, and which, to make it balance evenly, had been given four small feet by an angel. What was certain about Brigid was that from a very early age she loved God and wished to serve Him as a nun. Because of her beauty, many young noblemen wished to marry her, but she refused them all, and at last left her father's house, with some friends, to offer herself to do God's service in whatever way her bishop thought best. The bishop said, "You shall be called Sisters of Mercy," to give up their lives to serving God by prayer and works of charity.

Brigid and her companions chose as their first home a house under a great oak-tree, which they called Cill Dara – "the Church of Oak" - and which later grew into the city of Kildare. Her convent soon became the centre of religion and learning. She founded, too, a school of art, where metalwork and illumination of manuscripts was taught. The finest work produced there was an illuminated book of the Gospels, which disappeared at the Reformation but which those who saw it said had no equal. Every page was most gorgeously painted, with such elaborate designs, that according to an old chronicler the colours seemed "the work of angels, not human hands," and the story arose that night after night, as Brigid prayed, "an angel furnished the designs which the scribe copied."

The fame of Brigid spread far and wide. Her city of Kildare, with its Cathedral and its school, became famous all over Europe. She was known as Patroness of Ireland and "Queen of the South": and when she died the great shrine over her tomb was visited by pilgrims from all over Christendom.
Her Feast day is February 1st.

Question 10 ◆ What did Saint Brigid become as she grew older?
Question 11 ◆ What was the name of the city made famous by Saint Brigid?
Question 12 ◆ What did Saint Genevieve tell the people of Paris to do for the city to be saved from Attila?

Devotions

The Miraculous Medal

Some 28 years before Our Blessed Mother appeared to Saint Bernadette at Lourdes, she visited a Sister of Charity, Sister Catherine Laboure in a chapel in the Rue du Bac, Paris. At this apparition, Mary gave Saint Catherine Laboure the Miraculous Medal.

At the time of Benediction on 1st June 1830, she experienced a vision of Christ the King – at first majestic, but then sad. On the eve of the Feast of Saint Vincent de Paul (July 19), the Mother Superior, after speaking with the novices gave each a piece of cloth from the holy founder's surplice. Because of her extreme love, Catherine split her piece down the middle, swallowing half and placing the rest in her prayer book. She earnestly prayed to Saint Vincent that she might with her own eyes see the Mother of God. She was convinced that she would see the Blessed Virgin Mary that very night; and in her conviction, Catherine slept. Before long, she was awakened by a brilliant light and the voice of a beautiful child. "Sister Laboure, come to the chapel; the Blessed Virgin awaits you." Catherine replied: "We shall be discovered," The little angel smiled, "Do not be uneasy; it is half past 11; everyone is sleeping…… come, I am waiting for you." She rose quickly and dressed. The hall lights were burning. The locked chapel door swung open at the angel's touch. Amazed, she found the chapel ablaze with lights as if prepared for Midnight Mass. Quietly, she knelt at the Communion rail, and suddenly, she heard the rustle of a silk dress…. the Blessed Virgin, in a blaze of glory, sat in the Director's chair. The angel whispered: "The Blessed Mother wishes to speak with you."

Catherine rose, knelt beside the Blessed Mother, rested her hands in the Virgin's lap, and felt the Virgin's arms around her. Mary said: "God wishes to charge you with a mission. You will be contradicted, but do not fear; you will have the grace. Tell your spiritual director all that passes within you. Times are evil in France and in the world." A pain crossed the Virgin's face. "Come to the foot of the altar. Graces will be shed on all, great and little, especially upon those who seek them. Another community of sisters will join the Ru du Bac community. (This happened in 1849 when Father Etienne received Mother Elizabeth Seton's sisters of Emmitsburg, Maryland, into the Paris community. Mother Seton's sisters became the foundational stone of the Sisters of Charity in the United States.) The community will become large (there are 46,000 Sisters of Charity today; in 1830 there were 150 sisters); you will have the protection of Saint Vincent; I always will have my eyes upon you. There will be much persecution. The Cross will be treated with contempt; it will be hurled to the ground and blood will flow. The Archbishop will be stripped of his garments." Then, like a fading shadow, the Lady was gone.

Catherine arose, the child still hovered nearby. They left the chapel, marched up the corridor, and the angel disappeared. Catherine went to bed with the clock striking two.

This apparition was unlike any other apparition in the history of the world. Catherine expected it; a little angel beckoned her; the chapel was arranged in beauty, with flowers, candles, and lights ablaze, Catherine had the privilege of kneeling at Mary's knee and resting her hands on Mary's lap.

Level 4 - Lesson 4

General

Question 13 ◆ Why was this apparition so unlike any other apparition in the history of the world?

Question 14 ◆ To whom did Our Lady appear at the Rue du Bac?

Question 15 ◆ Why do people go to Lourdes today?

The Ecclesiastical Year

In the last lesson we studied the feasts of the Church. In addition to the feasts which occur throughout the year, we have what is called the Ecclesiastical Year, which is made up of six seasons or periods of unequal length:

1. Advent — A period of preparation for Christmas
2. Christmastide — The season of celebration after Christmas, a season of joy
3. Septuagesima — A period of preparation for Lent
4. Lent — The period of penance preceding Easter
5. Pascal Time — The time from Easter till the eve of Trinity Sunday
6. Time after Pentecost — The period after Pentecost; the longest of the liturgical seasons, varying between 23 and 28 weeks

Unlike our civil year which commences on the first day of January, the Ecclesiastical Year (or Liturgical Year) begins with the First Sunday of Advent; four Sundays before Christmas.

It is important to live the Church Year, to enter into the spirit of each of the Liturgical Seasons; to do penance during Lent, to rejoice during Pascal Time etc. Learn well the six seasons of the Church.

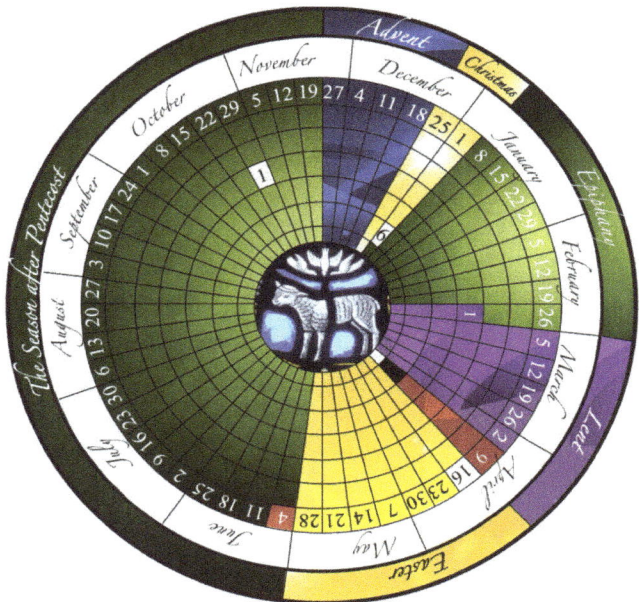

Question 16 ◆ What are the six seasons of the Church (in order)?
Question 17 ◆ What are the four divisions of Feast Days?

Lesson 5

Level 4

Pre - Confirmation

Catechism

The Third Commandment

101. What is the third commandment of God?

    The Third commandment of God is: Remember thou keep holy the Lord's day.

102. What are we commanded by the third commandment?

    By the third commandment we are commanded to worship God in a special manner on Sunday, the Lord's day.

103. How does the Church command us to worship God on Sunday?

    The Church commands us to worship God on Sunday by assisting at the Holy Sacrifice of the Mass.

104. What is forbidden by the third commandment of God?

    By the third commandment of God all unnecessary servile work on Sunday is forbidden.

105. What is servile work?

    Servile work is that which requires labour of body rather than of mind.

God made the world in six days and on the seventh day He rested. He wants us too, to rest on the seventh day and to make it holy by going to Mass in particular. The world today has forgotten God, or worse, has turned away from God. For many people, alas, even Catholics, Sunday is just another day.

How many people go shopping on a Sunday? How many people mow the lawns on Sunday? These things are forbidden and yet so many Catholics still do them. Let us be very careful to keep Sunday holy. Ask Saint John Marie Vianney to remind you. He spend many years preaching to his parish, teaching them to make holy the Lord's Day.

Question 1 ◆ What are we commanded by the third commandment?
Question 2 ◆ What is forbidden by the third commandment of God?
Question 3 ◆ What is cursing?

Level 4 - Lesson 5

Prayer

The Hail Mary

We have just completed four lessons on the Our Father, the prayer that Jesus Himself taught us. Over the next few lessons we are going to learn the meaning of the Hail Mary, perhaps the prayer we say more often than any other prayer. In fact, each time we pray the Rosary we say the Hail Mary 53 times.

Hail Mary, full of Grace

This was the greeting of the Angel Gabriel when he asked Mary to be the Mother of Jesus. It is our greeting too each time we pray to our dear Mother. We acknowledge that she is full of grace. If a salt container is full of salt, there is no room for any pepper. Our Lady's soul is full of grace; there is no room at all for sin. There have been many holy people throughout the ages, but it is only to Mary that we can say, Full of Grace.

The Lord is with thee

From the time of Mary's Conception (the Immaculate Conception) God was with Our Lady. She has never sinned and God is always with her. Alas, we sometimes fall into mortal sin and God is forced to leave our souls, this was never the case with Mary. Of course, after Mary said yes to the angel, the Lord was also physically present in the womb of Mary – this was the Incarnation.

Question 4 ◆ Who was conceived immaculately?
Question 5 ◆ What do we mean by the Incarnation?
Question 6 ◆ What are we asking of God when we pray the words, And lead us not into temptation?

Bible Story

Jesus Before His Enemies

Jesus Before the High Priest

The crowd led Jesus to the house of a Priest, named Annas, who asked Jesus many questions, and Jesus answered that He had not taught in secret. For saying this, one of Annas' servants gave Jesus a blow across the face.

Peter Denies Jesus

When Jesus was in the house of Annas, Peter was outside in the court-yard of the house, where there was a fire burning, for it was cold, and about him were many people, soldiers and servants. While Peter stood at the fire very sad, a servant woman came to warm herself also, and said: "This man was with Him;" but Peter said: "Woman, I know Him not." After a little while, a man said: "Of a truth, this man was also with Him." Then Peter again, with many strong words, said: "Man, I know not what thou sayest." Then as he denied Jesus a third time, the cock crew. Jesus was then passing through the court of Caiaphas, the High Priest, to whom Annas had sent Him, and He turned and looked at Peter. Peter then remembered what Jesus had said, that he would deny Him three times before the cock crew, and "Peter, going out, wept bitterly." The men that held Jesus struck Him cruel blows, jeering at Him, and crying out: "Say who it is that has struck you?" but Jesus remained silent.

Caiaphas

Jesus, when He was before Caiaphas, was asked if He was "the Christ, the Son of God?" and Jesus answered: "I am Caiaphas did not believe this, and said it was a wicked thing to say, and gave Jesus up into the hands of the people, to be taken the next day to the ruler, Pilate.

Question 7	◆	Why did the servant of Annas hit Jesus across the face?
Question 8	◆	How many times did Saint Peter deny Jesus?
Question 9	◆	When Jesus went and prayed, what did His Apostles do?

The Saints

Saint Giles

Giles lived alone in a cave deep in a wild forest, not far from where the river Rhone flows into the Mediterranean Sea. He had, after many travels, made his home there so that he might escape from people who thought he was a saint. One day, as he was going into church, he had noticed a poor, sick beggar lying on the pavement outside; and to make him more comfortable he had taken off his own cloak and spread it over him. The man had been immediately healed, and the crowds started to gather and call Giles a holy man.

But Giles knew that the healing had nothing to do with his own goodness. He remembered, too, that when the people had surrounded Jesus after He had performed one of His miracles He had escaped from them and gone away alone into a deserted place to pray to God. Giles determined to try to do the same, not because he did not want to help the sick and the suffering, but because he thought the best way to do it was by hiding himself from the world and spending his time in prayer for it.

So he became a hermit in the forest of Nimes; and no one knew of his cave by the side of a clear spring, which gave him water to drink, as the trees and plants round about gave him herbs and fruits to eat. But he had one companion, a little hind who had become tame and made her home with him.

One day, when the King of that part of France was hunting in the forest, the hind was pursued by the huntsmen and dogs, and in terror it fled to the cave and took refuge in Giles' arms. The prayers of the holy man caused thick bushes to spring up as a protection, so that the hounds were baffled. But one of the huntsmen shot an arrow in the direction the hind had taken, and when at last they found their way to the cave they discovered that the arrow had wounded, not the hind, but Giles. When they saw this the King and his huntsmen were very sorry. They knelt and asked the hermit's forgiveness; but Giles, who realised it was an accident, said there was nothing to forgive. They offered to bind the wound; but Giles explained that it was of no account. The King implored him to come with him to court; but Giles told him that nothing would make him leave the way of life that he had chosen for the glory of God. So at last they left him alone and returned to the chase. But now that he had discovered so famous a holy man living in his dominions the King could not let the matter rest. He went back to Giles and asked that, if he would not come to court, at least he would allow some people who were also trying to live a good life to come and live near him. Giles realized that this was his duty to God.

About a hundred and fifty years earlier, Saint Benedict had gone away to serve God in the desert just as Giles had; but in the end he had allowed others who wished to serve God in the same way to come and live with him under a strict Rule of Life which he drew up for them. By Giles' day there were many monasteries in Europe under this Benedictine Rule; and Giles, after much prayer and thought, told the King that if he would build a Benedictine monastery near his cave he would become abbot of it.

This the King did; and though Giles himself never left his cave and at last died in it, the great Abbey of Saint Giles which was built there in the forest became one of the greatest homes for monks in France. His Feast day is September 1st.

Level 4 - Lesson 5

The Saints

Question 10   ◆   Why did Saint Giles go and live in a cave in the forest?
Question 11   ◆   What was the name of the monastery built by the King near the cave of Saint Giles?
Question 12   ◆   What was the name of the city made famous by Saint Brigid?

Devotions

The Miraculous Medal
(Continued)

Little Catherine lived a normal life until Advent. On Saturday, 27 November 1830, at 5:30 p.m., she retired to the chapel with the other nuns for evening meditation. Catherine heard the faint swish of silk, she recognised Our Lady's signal. Raising her eyes to the main altar, she saw her beautiful Lady standing on a large globe. Mary's silken robe shone with the whiteness of dawn; the neck was cut high, and the sleeves were plain. A pure white veil fell to her feet, and beneath the veil she wore a lace fillet binding her hair. A small golden ball was in her hands, which she offered to God with her eyes heavenwards.

Suddenly, Mary's hands were resplendent and flashed in a brilliant cascade of light. The flood of glory was so bright that the globe on which Mary stood was out of sight. Catherine understood that the rays symbolised the graces shed on those who seek; gems on Our Lady's fingers which did not have rays symbolised the graces for which souls forget to ask. Then the ball vanished.

Mary's arms swept wide and down, and an oval frame of words surrounded her head O Mary, conceived without sin, pray for us who have recourse to thee.

The Virgin spoke again, this time giving a direct order: "Have a medal struck in this form. All who wear it will receive great graces." Then the vision of the Virgin turned completely around, and on the other side appeared a huge letter M with a cross above it. The letter rested on a bar, beneath which appeared two hearts. The first heart was encircled by a crown of thorns; the second was pierced by a sword. The explanation is simple. We are Christians, repurchased by a God who was crucified in the very presence of His own mother, the Queen of Martyrs.

Question 13 ◆ On what date did Saint Catherine receive the Miraculous Medal?
Question 14 ◆ Describe, as accurately as possible (without drawing) the Miraculous Medal.
Question 15 ◆ Why was this apparition so unlike any other apparition in the history of the world?

General

The Commandments of the Church

A bad Catholic once said to a friend, "God will not punish me for not keeping the Church laws. I observe all the Ten Commandments and I do not need to obey the laws made only by the Church." But the friend answered, "Did not God command us to listen to the Church? Then if we do not obey its laws, we disobey Him as well."

The Catholic Church has the right to make laws from Jesus Christ, Who said to the Apostles, "Whatsoever you bind on earth shall be bound also in heaven." The right to make laws is exercised by the bishops, the successors of the Apostles, and especially by the Pope, who as the successor of the chief of Apostles, Saint Peter, has the right to make laws for the universal Church.

The Pope can make and unmake laws for the entire Church; his authority is supreme and unquestioned. Every bishop, every priest, every member of the Church is subject to him.

Laws are also made by each bishop for his own diocese, and by a general council of bishops for the entire Church. These last have no power without the Pope's approval.

A good Catholic shows obedience to God by strictly obeying what the Church commands. The Church is our Mother, good and wise, who looks only to our temporal and spiritual welfare; let us show our love for her by the obedience we render.

The Church has many commandments or laws which are contained in what is called the Code of Canon Law, but there are six chief commandments or laws, namely:

1) To assist at Mass on all Sundays and holy days of obligation.
2) To fast and to abstain on the days appointed.
3) To confess our sins at least once a year.
4) To receive Holy Communion during the Easter season.
5) To contribute to the support of the Church.
6) To observe the laws of the Church concerning marriage.

Question 16 ◆ How many chief Commandments of the Church are there?
Question 17 ◆ List the chief Commandments of the Church
Question 18 ◆ Why should we obey the Church?

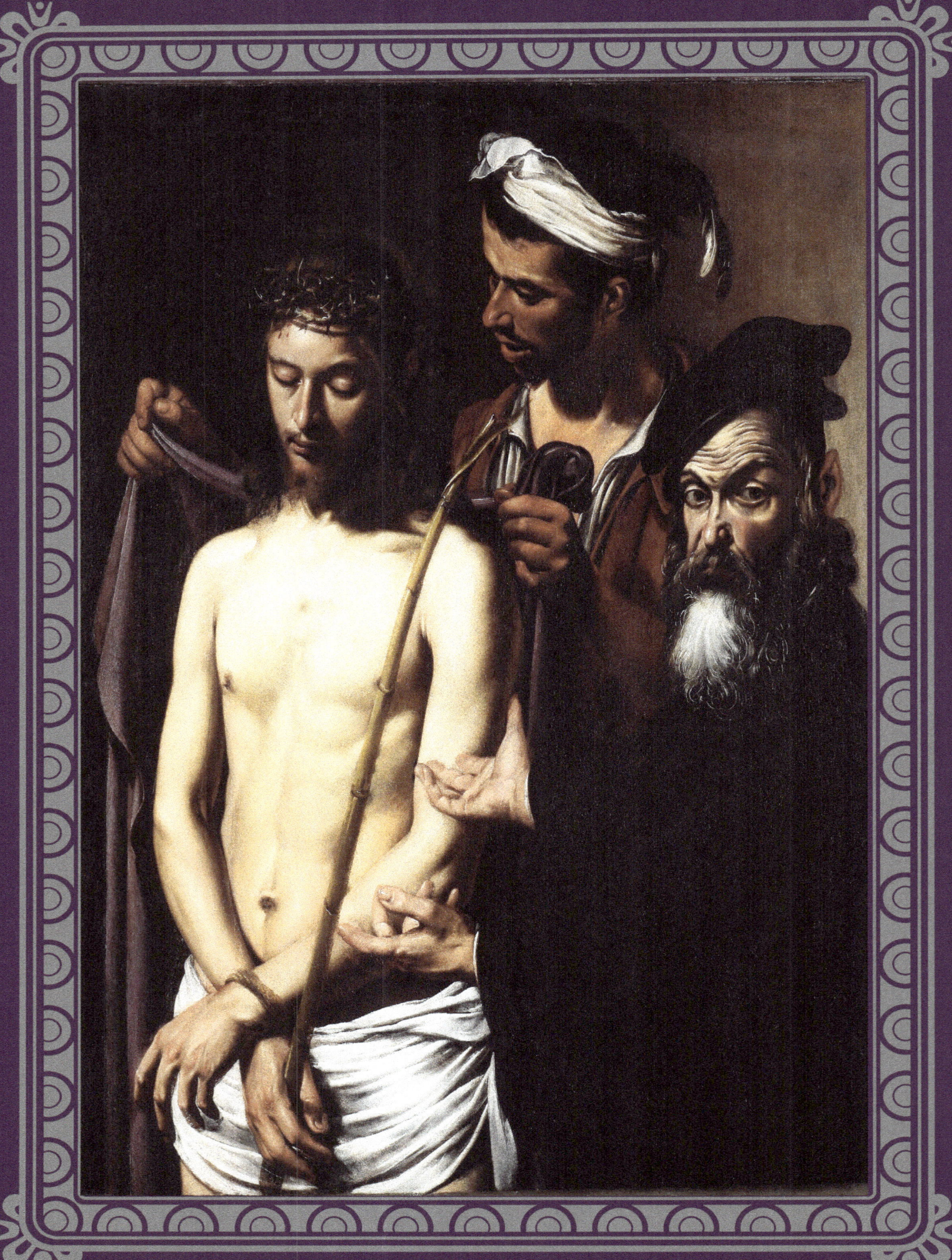

Lesson 6

Level 4

Pre - Confirmation

Catechism

The Fourth Commandment

106. What is the fourth commandment of God?

The fourth commandment of God is: Honour thy father and thy mother.

107. What are we commanded by the fourth commandment?

By the fourth commandment we are commanded to respect and love our parents, to obey them in all that is not sinful, and to help them when they are in need.

108. What does the fourth commandment forbid?

The fourth commandment forbids disrespect, unkindness, and disobedience to our parents and lawful superiors.

The first three Commandments deal principally with our relationship with God; the last seven Commandments deal with our relationship with our neighbour. The fourth Commandment commands us to respect and obey our parents and lawful superiors. This is not solely a commandment for young children; we all have superiors, and as far as they do not lead us into sin, or away from God, we are bound to obey them.

Question 1 ◆ What are we commanded by the fourth commandment?
Question 2 ◆ What does the fourth commandment forbid?
Question 3 ◆ How does the Church command us to worship God on Sunday?

Prayer

The Hail Mary (continued…)

Blessed art thou among women

When Our Lady came to visit her cousin Elizabeth, (Saint John the Baptist was to be born three months later), she greeted Mary with the above words, Blessed art thou among women. Truly, Our Lady is blessed above all of God's creatures. Of all people, she is the only one that sin never touched (excepting Jesus Himself, Who is God). From the moment of her conception, she was preserved free from Original Sin. Why? Because she was to be the Mother of God; the most singular privilege ever given to any creature. Meditate upon these things when saying these words in the Hail Mary.

And blessed is the fruit of thy womb, Jesus.

Saint Elizabeth was not only shown the greatness of Mary, but God revealed to her, He who was to be born of the Virgin Mary. She knew that the babe in the womb of Mary was the Christ, the Promised One when she said the words, And blessed is the fruit of thy womb. It was the Church which added the name Jesus to the prayer.

Question 4 ◆ The words, Blessed art thou among women and blessed is the fruit of thy womb, came from whom?

Question 5 ◆ Who added the word Jesus to this part of the Hail Mary?

Question 6 ◆ What do we mean by the Incarnation?

Bible Story

The Scourging at the Pillar

Jesus was brought by the people to Pilate, who asked what he had done; and when Jesus had answered, he said: "I find no fault in the man;" but the people only cried out all the more that Jesus was a disturber. Now, it was a feast-day, and it was the custom on those days, as an act of mercy, to release some man who was imprisoned for his crimes. So Pilate, who wished to make peace with the people, and, perhaps get the release of Jesus, said to them: "There is in prison a man named Barabbas, a murderer; shall I release him to you, or shall I release Jesus?" The people said, "Let us have Barabbas, and crucify Jesus." But Pilate said to them: "Why, what evil hath He done?" But they cried out the more: "Crucify Him." So Pilate released Barabbas, and gave Jesus up to them.

Pilate thought that if he made Jesus suffer, the people's hearts would be touched and he could save Him; so he had Jesus scourged. Do you know what this word scourged means? It means whipped or flogged. But such a painful flogging! - you cannot imagine it!

Question 7 ◆ Who did the Jews ask to be released in the place of Jesus?
Question 8 ◆ Why did Pilate have Jesus scourged?
Question 9 ◆ Why did the servant of Annas hit Jesus across the face?

The Saints

Saint Bernard of Clairvaux

About the year 1100AD, certain monks decided that they would try to live again strictly according to the old Rule, and they went off into a lonely place called Citeaux to found a new monastery. They took their name from the place and were known as Cistercians; but the life they led was so hard that, one after another, the monks left, and it seemed that the monastery would have to close.

Then one evening in the year 1113, just as the monks were going to bed, there was a loud knocking at the gate. The Abbot, who was an Englishman named Stephen Harding, ordered it to be opened and saw standing there about thirty men. He did not know whether they were robbers or travelers.

"Do you come in peace?" he asked.
"The peace of God," answered the young man of twenty-two who seemed to be the leader.
"Then, you are welcome to stay here for the night."
"If you will have us, Father," said the young man, "we have come to stay forever."
Then he explained that his name was Bernard, the son of the Lord of Fontaines, one of the leading nobles of Burgundy, and that with him were some of his five brothers and other relations as well as friends. They all wished to become monks at Citeaux.
"My children," said the Abbot, "even if I could refuse you I would not, for this is the Lord's doing and marvelous in our eyes. You have come at a moment when I was near to despair. It seemed that we were defeated and that the world was laughing at us. And now God has sent you in answer to our prayers and faith. Yet I must warn you that life here in the service of God is a life of hardship, having little comfort, needing no less bravery than a soldier needs who faces the dangers of war."

"I know, and they know," said Bernard. "Many of them have been soldiers."
So Bernard and his companions put on the white robe of the Cistercians, and for two years they stayed at Citeaux, until at the end of that time Abbot Stephen sent twelve of them under Bernard's leadership to found a new house. The place they chose was by a river in the woods, which was known as the Valley of Bitterness. With Bernard went his four brothers, Gerard and Guy and Andrew and Bartholomew, his uncle Gauldry, and his young cousin Robert.

It was very hard work, for first they had to make a clearing in the woods before they could set up the first rough building, from which in time the monastery would grow. They cut down trees for timber; they made their bricks from clay they baked on the spot; and their roof was a thatch of rushes. They had taken with them a little supply of barley and millet, from which they made some coarse black bread; and they made soup of beech-leaves soaked in water with a little salt.

Level 4 - Lesson 6

The Saints

One day they found that they had hardly any bread left and no salt, so Bernard sent one of his brothers off to the nearest town to get some.

"Can I have some money to buy it with?" he asked.

"When have we ever had money since we left home?" said Bernard. "Go and ask in God's name, and in God's name it will be given you."

At the edge of the wood the brother met a priest, who asked him where he was going. On being told, the priest said that his people would be only too glad to help the monks, and at once sent over half a barrel of salt and plenty of bread for them all.

When at last the house was built Bernard changed the name of the place where it stood. Now it was no longer the Valley of Bitterness. It was the Valley of Light – Clairvaux. And that is why he is always know in history as Bernard of Clairvaux.

But soon Clairvaux was too small to hold all the people who came to it asking to be monks there. Bernard's own father was one of those who came. The monastery grew famous, and Bernard himself became the friend and adviser of kings and bishops. Once the Pope himself visited Clairvaux, but, although that was a very great occasion, the simple Rule was not altered. The best meal the monks could give him was bread and a few fish and, instead of wine, the juice of herbs.

Besides his work as an abbot and his preaching, Bernard was a great writer; and one of his Latin hymns, Jesu dulcis memoria, which in English begins, "Jesus, the very thought of Thee with sweetness fills my breast," is still sung all over the world.

Question 10   ◆   Why was the Abbot Stephen Harding so pleased to see Saint Bernard and his companions?
Question 11   ◆   What does the word Clairvaux mean?
Question 12   ◆   Why did Saint Giles go and live in a cave in the forest?

Devotions

The Miraculous Medal (continued)

Catherine asked how she was to have the medal struck. Mary replied that she was to go to her confessor, Father Jean Marie Aladel (born 4 May 1800), saying: "He is my servant."

Father Aladel at first did not believe Catherine; however, after two years, he finally went to the Archbishop who ordered 2,000 medals struck on 30 June 1832. There was in Paris a renegade Archbishop who had sided with Napoleon against the Holy See and who had been excommunicated. The legal Archbishop went to the bedside of the dying renegade. Through the Miraculous Medal which the good Archbishop left, the renegade confessed; his soul passed to heaven the next day.

Pope Gregory XVI placed one of the medals at the foot of the crucifix on his desk. Catherine continued to live a solid religious life, taking care of the English Home for the Aged near Rue du Bac. While Catherine continues to keep her secret, only relating her visions to her confessor, let us briefly review the medal and Ratisbonne.

A Dare and a Conversion

Alfonse Tobie Ratisbonne was a wealthy Jewish lawyer and banker of Strasbourg, who above all hated Catholicism. While traveling to Malta, his ship was delayed. He went to Rome to rest and become more than ever disgusted with Catholicism. A friend gave him a medal, daring him to wear it and to say the Memorare. He went to the Church of Saint Andrea delle Fratte with a friend to make funeral arrangements for another friend. At the front door, a menacing black dog frisked at him ...the dog vanished. Then a brilliant light came from the Guardian Angel Chapel, and he saw Mary as on the Miraculous Medal. He was converted on the spot, begging immediate baptism. However, such was not granted, but after instructions, the Jesuits baptized him at the Gesu in Rome. Alfonse then became a Jesuit scholastic, and after 10 years, he asked to go to China but was refused. With permission, he left the Society of Jesus and joined the Congregation of Our Lady of Sion for the evangelization of the Jews. For 30 years he laboured in the Holy Land to his own people.

Catherine, in the meantime, suffering arthritis, knelt ever attentive in chapel for long hours. In spite of this, she accomplished her ordinary daily duties in an extraordinary manner. As the years rolled on, she became portress where she sewed away the hours between visits of those who called. Asthma set in, and soon blood letting.

General

Level 4 - Lesson 6

After 46 years, her confessor advised her to reveal the story of the apparitions – her secret that she was the nun to whom the Blessed Mother appeared – to her Mother Superior so that a proper statue might be sculptured.

On the last day of December 1876 she passed on – once again into the arms of Mary – this time however, in heaven. Today, her beautiful remains still lie fresh and serene; her eyes are a brilliant blue; her arms and legs are supple; she does not seem dead.

Question 13 ◆ At first, did Saint Catherine's confessor believe her?
Question 14 ◆ What happened to Saint Catherine's body after she died?
Question 15 ◆ Describe, as accurately as possible (without drawing) the Miraculous Medal.

The Four Last Things

The purpose of our existence is that we give honour and glory to God and thereby save our souls. In fact, we are born to die. Our whole eternity depends upon the moment of our death. Of course our death will be the result of the lives we lead.

The Church reminds us therefore of the four last things to be ever remembered:

> Death
> Judgment
> Heaven
> Hell

We are all certain that we will die; we do not know when or how, but we know it will happen. The poorest servant and the greatest king are subject to death; the result of Original Sin. When we die, we will face God's judgment. Depending upon the state of our soul at the moment of our death will be determined our eternal destiny. We know we cannot avoid death, nor can we escape God's judgment.

At the moment of judgment, our souls will either fly to heaven to enjoy eternal bliss (possibly via the fires of Purgatory) or be cast into the everlasting fires of hell.

We know we will die and be judged. If we correspond with God's grace, we will enjoy an eternity of happiness with Him. If we refuse His graces, we are lost forever. How we live we will die.

Question 16 ◆ What are the four last things ever to be remembered?
Question 17 ◆ What two things can we not escape before we either go to heaven or hell?

Lesson 7

Level 4

Pre - Confirmation

Catechism

The Fifth Commandment

109. What is the fifth commandment of God?

The fifth commandment of God is: Thou shalt not kill.

110. What are we commanded by the fifth commandment?

By the fifth commandment we are commanded to take proper care of our own spiritual and bodily well-being and that of our neighbour.

111. What does the fifth commandment forbid?

The fifth commandment forbids murder and suicide, and also fighting, anger, hatred, revenge, drunkenness, reckless driving, and bad example.

When we examine our conscience on the Fifth Commandment, we often pass it by very quickly, thinking that, having never killed anybody, we have done nothing to break God's law in this regard. Read very well, Question 111. This commandment forbids much more that just killing, but uncontrolled anger, hatred and so on. This Commandment is broken much more often than we think. Thus we need to examine ourselves more carefully on it.

Question 1 ◆ What are we commanded by the fifth commandment?
Question 2 ◆ What does the fifth commandment forbid?
Question 3 ◆ What does the fourth commandment forbid?

Level 4 - Lesson 7

Prayer

The Hail Mary (continued...)

Holy Mary, Mother of God

The second part of the Hail Mary was composed by the Church. The angel greeted Mary with, Full of Grace. We now greet her as the Mother of God. She does not just have the title of Mother of Jesus (in His human nature), but the Mother of God. What a glorious title!

We will study next lesson the petitions in the Hail Mary; the things we ask for. With what confidence we can ask Mary because she is the holy Mother of God.

Question 4 ◆ Under what title do we pray to Mary in the Hail Mary?

Bible Story

The Crowning With Thorns

After that dreadful scourging, the Roman soldiers put an old purple dress upon Jesus, a reed in His hand, and on His head a crown of thorns. They made Jesus a mock king. Coming up to Him, they mocked Him, and bending down before Him, said: "Hail, King of the Jews." Then they spat at Him, and struck Him, pressing the thorns deep into His head by their blows. How it must have hurt Jesus! How He suffered for those bad thoughts we have sometimes! Often when you are asked why you have done a bad thing, you will say, "I don't know; it came into my head." When these things come into your head, think for a moment of the crown of thorns on the head of Jesus, and you will not do wrong.

Pilate and the Jews

When Pilate saw what a dreadful state Jesus was in after all this cruel work, he thought that if he was to show Jesus to the people they would have pity; so he led Jesus out on a balcony, and said to the people: "Behold the man!" but they had no pity, and cried out: "Crucify Him." Pilate saw it was of no use to try to save Jesus, but he was afraid to lose the favour of the people, and said to them: "He is a just man." Then he called for a basin, and washed his hands before the people, to show that his hands were clean of the death of Jesus. And he said to them: "I am innocent of the blood of this just man; look you to it." And the people cried out: "His blood be upon us, and upon our children." Pilate then said Jesus was to die, and gave Him up to the Jews.

Question 5	◆	Why did the soldiers crown Jesus with thorns?
Question 6	◆	What did Pilate say when he saw Jesus after He was crowned?
Question 7	◆	Who did the Jews ask to be released in the place of Jesus?

The Saints

Saint Joan of Arc

Jaques D'Arc – or, as we should call him in English, James of Arc – was a farmer in the little village of Domremy. He had five children, of whom the youngest was named Joan. When she was a small girl she used to help to look after her father's sheep, and as she got older she learnt to sew and spin for the family; but, like Saint Genevieve long before her, she would often go away alone to think about God and to say her prayers. And, just as happened with Saint Genevieve, God sent angels and messengers to talk to her.

She was thirteen when she first heard her "voices," as she called them. She was in her father's garden when there was a great light beside her, and out of the light spoke a voice which she thought was the Archangel Michael. Saint Michael, she knew, was the leader of the warrior-angels, for she had heard often the passage from the Bible which tells how Saint Michael was God's champion in the war against Satan.

And it was not surprising that the warrior-angel should have been chosen to give a message about the terrible war which was going on in France at the time. For nearly a hundred years, there had been war between the English and the French. The English kings had said that they ought to be kings of France too, and had come with armies to try to conquer France. No one in France could live in safety, because soldiers went about the countryside robbing and destroying. There was no law. Even Paris was in the hands of the enemy, and the true King of France, Charles, had not been able to be crowned.

The message which Saint Michael gave to Joan was that God had seen "the great misery of France" and had chosen her to put an end to it. The last part was so surprising that Joan could hardly believe it, and for four years she said nothing about it to anyone. But during those four years the voices still came to her, and other saints besides Saint Michael appeared to her; while in the country the war got worse and worse. Charles, the Dauphin-for until he had been anointed with the holy oil at his coronation he could not be called King-was preparing to leave the country. The English were besieging Orleans, and when it was taken they would be masters of France. All hope would have gone.

So, when she was seventeen-it was the beginning of the year 1429-Joan knew she must wait no longer. She must obey the voices that God had sent her, even though what they ordered her to do was something no girl had ever done before.

Saint Genevieve had lived through times when France was overrun by foreign armies, and she had done it by becoming a nun and offering her prayers and by helping and encouraging people when they were afraid. But Joan was told to act quite differently and in a way that everyone would say was mad. She, who had barely been out of her village, was to go and find the Dauphin and have him crowned. She, who was a simple peasant girl, to drive the English out of France.

"I am only a poor girl," she said to her voices. "I do not know how to ride and fight."

"It is God who commands it," they answered.

So she set out, and though the officer to whom she first went to ask him to take her to the Dauphin said, "Take her home to her father and give her a good whipping," she persevered until at last she got to the Court at Chinon.

The Saints

Here too they thought she was mad and played a trick on her. The Dauphin told one of the courtiers to dress up in the royal clothes while he himself pretended to be one of the courtiers. But Joan, though she had never seen him before, came straight up to him and told him why she had come. When he still hesitated she whispered to him a secret which the voices had told her; something which no one in the world except himself knew. That made him change his mind and, though many of his courtiers still tried to prevent it, he let Joan have her way. Dressed in a suit of armour, mounted on a white horse, and bearing a white banner with the words "Jesus: Mary" on it, she rode at the head of the French army to Orleans, which was surrounded by English troops. She ordered the attack and drove the enemy away from the city. There were other battles, which she won; and at last she was able to take the Dauphin safely to Reims, where in the great cathedral he was anointed and crowned King. Then she went back to fighting the English.

The English troops did not think she was mad. They thought she was a witch who had got her strange power from Satan, and when in a battle her enemies managed to capture her they brought her to trial for witchcraft.

Her enemies shut her up in a dungeon; they kept her chained to a great log of wood; they did not allow her to receive Holy Communion; and they questioned her again and again to try to make her say that her voices did not really come from God. The ungrateful King made no attempt to rescue her; even some priests and bishops tried to make her believe she had done wrong and that her voices were either her imagination or evil spirits; in the end they burnt her at the stake in Rouen.

But Joan, though she was only nineteen, was as brave and as certain before her judges as she had been on the battlefield. Whatever she did, she knew she must be faithful to God. And when an English soldier, who had tied together two sticks in the form of a cross so that she might have it to hold as she was dying, said "God have pity on us, for we have burnt a saint," he was telling the truth. Saint Joan of Arc's Feast Day is May 30th.

Question 8 ◆ How old was Saint Joan of Arc when she first heard her voices
Question 9 ◆ What was St Joan of Arc asked to do to save France?
Question 10 ◆ What does the word Clairvaux mean?

Devotions

The Story of Fatima

Our Blessed Mother appeared to three shepherd children in 1917. Jacinta was seven, Francisco was nine and Lucia was ten. Over the next few lessons we will study the apparition at Fatima and more importantly, we will learn the lessons that Our Lady taught us, principally, prayer and penance.

In 1916, Lucia, Francisco and Jacinta were looking after their flocks when suddenly an angel appeared to them. He was resplendent and was very close to them. He said that he was the Angel of Peace. He taught them some prayers which the children learnt and prayed daily.

Three times the angel appeared to the children. On the third occasion, he gave them Holy Communion. Oh what joy the children experienced in this! These visits of the angel were a preparation for something far greater: the visit of Our Lady herself.

At noon, on the 13th May, 1917, the children knelt to say the Rosary in the meadow (Cova da Iria) where they were tending their sheep. A beautiful lady dressed in white appeared to them. She told the children not to be afraid, she was from heaven. She asked them to come to the same place at the same time for six successive months. At every visit she asked the children to say the Rosary every day.

A month later, on the 13th June, with some people present, the children waited for Our Lady to appear again. Once again, she descended upon the holm oak tree. She asked Lucia to learn to read. In her right hand she held a heart surrounded by thorns which pierced it. They understood it was the Immaculate Heart of Mary, outraged by the sins of Humanity, and that she wished for Reparation. On the 13th July, Our Lady gave the same message: 'Continue to say the Rosary daily, in honour of Our Lady, in order to obtain peace in the world and the end of the war, because only she can obtain it.' She promised that in October she would tell who she was and what she wanted; she would perform a miracle so that all would believe. The children had been having a hard time because many people thought they were telling lies and making up fancy stories. It was at this apparition Our Lady asked for sacrifices for sinners and for the children to say: Oh Jesus, it is for love of Thee, for the conversion of sinners and in reparation for the sins committed against the Immaculate Heart of Mary. She gave the children a vision of Hell and predicted the terrible things to happen in the world if men did not stop offending God. It was at this time that Our Lady taught the children the Decade Prayer that we all say after each decade of the Rosary: Oh my Jesus, forgive us our sins, save us from the fire of hell, lead all souls to heaven, especially those in most need of Thy mercy.

Question 11 ♦ In what year did Our Lady appear at Fatima?
Question 12 ♦ What did the lady show the children in July?
Question 13 ♦ Our Lady had two main messages to the children. What were they?
Question 14 ♦ What happened to Saint Catherine's body after she died?

General

Level 4 - Lesson 7

The Four Marks of the Church

In the Credo (Creed) we pray: One, Holy, Catholic and Apostolic Church. These are the Four Marks of the Church. Our Lord started the Church. He said, "Thou art Peter, and upon this rock I will build my Church".

The devil wants to destroy the Church by any means he can. He has started up many false churches – be they Christian or otherwise. The Bible tells us that all other churches are of the devil.

So how can we tell the true Church of Jesus Christ from the increasing number of false churches? By the four marks of the Church.

The Catholic Church is One: No matter where in the world you live, the belief is the same, the Mass is the same, the Sacraments are the same. The Church is one in its belief and doctrine.

The Catholic Church is Holy: Its founder is holy, its doctrine is holy and it leads souls to holiness.

The Catholic Church is Catholic: This means 'Universal'. It is for all people in all places for all times. It is the same Church today as it was 1,000 years ago.

The Catholic Church is Apostolic: The bishops/priests of the Catholic Church today are in a direct line from the Apostles.

Only the Catholic Church is ONE, HOLY, CATHOLIC and APOSTOLIC. No other church has these four things.

The Four Marks of the Church

One

Holy

Catholic

Apostolic

Question 15 ◆ What are the four marks of the Church?
Question 16 ◆ What do we mean when we say the Church is Apostolic?
Question 17 ◆ What do we mean when we say the Church is One?
Question 18 ◆ What are the four last things ever to be remembered?

Lesson 8

Level 4

Pre - Confirmation

Catechism

The Sixth Commandment

112. What is the sixth commandment?

The sixth commandment of God is: Thou shalt not commit adultery.

113. What are we commanded by the sixth commandment?

By the sixth commandment we are commanded to be pure and modest in our behavior.

114. What does the sixth commandment forbid?

The sixth commandment forbids all impurity and immodesty in words, looks, and actions, whether alone or with others.

Our Lady said at Fatima that more souls go to hell because of sins of impurity than any other sin. Thus, more souls go to hell because they break the sixth (and ninth) commandments than any of the other commandments.

These commandments bid us be pure in every thought and action. We live in a world today that is immoral and impure to the core. One cannot walk down the street without being confronted by impurity; the newspapers are full of it, the radio speaks of it constantly and the television and movies are a cesspool of immorality. Yet God gives us the graces we need to be pure.

Question 1 ◆ What are we commanded by the sixth commandment?
Question 2 ◆ What does the sixth commandment forbid?

Level 4 - Lesson 8

Prayer

The Hail Mary (continued…)

Pray for us sinners

We pray to Our Blessed Mother to help us because we are sinners and she is free from sin. She, who sits on the throne as Queen of Heaven and Earth; she whose intercession before God is so powerful, because she is indeed the Mother of God, and God will refuse her nothing. We beg our dear Mother to pray for us because we admit that we are sinners and we need her motherly intercession.

Now and at the hour of our death.

We ask Our Lady to never forget us; in our present needs, but also at the moment of our death. He who has Mary as his mother during life, will have her as his queen for eternity. Foster a strong and true devotion to Mary and she will protect you under her mantle. Amen.

So be it.

Remember, when ever you pray the words of the Hail Mary, do not do so as a parrot, saying words you neither understand nor mean. Meditate upon these sacred words and beg Mary to help you love Jesus more and more.

Question 3	◆	Why do we ask Mary to pray for us at our death?
Question 4	◆	What petition are we asking of Our Blessed Mother in the Hail Mary?
Question 5	◆	Under what title do we pray to Mary in the Hail Mary?

Bible Story

The Journey to Calvary

At that time it was the Roman custom to crucify people who were ordered to be killed for great crimes. In some countries they hang people, and in France they used to cut off their heads, but in the country where our Saviour lived they crucified, that is, nailed, and tied a person to a cross until he died.

Jesus, then, all weak and torn and bleeding, was led out of Pilate's house by the soldiers, and they made Him carry on His shoulders the cross on which He was to die.

What a sad sight it must have been for Mary, His mother, and His disciples and friends to see! Even the women and children of the Jews cried for very pity, when they saw Jesus bending under the weight of the great cross He was carrying. Jesus turned to these poor women, and said: "Daughters of Jerusalem, weep not over Me: but weep for yourselves and for your children."

The place to which Jesus had to carry His cross was called Calvary. With Jesus were two wicked men who were also going to Calvary to be put to death. Jesus was so weak when He was carrying His cross that He fell down three times. At last He could carry it no further, and the soldiers made a man named Simon, who was passing by, help to carry the cross the rest of the way.

Question 6 ◆ What was the Roman custom of putting people to death?
Question 7 ◆ How many times did Jesus fall on His way to Calvary?
Question 8 ◆ What did Pilate say when he saw Jesus after He was crowned?

The Saints

Saint Jerome Emiliani

Jerome Emiliani was born in Venice in 1481. His father died while he was still a boy, and when he was fifteen he decided to become a soldier in the army that Venice was raising against attack by the other nations of Europe. The Republic of Venice, which included much land round the city itself, had many towns that other nations wanted, and the French and the Spanish and the Germans were joining together in a league against it. So Jerome, like so many other Venetians, felt it was his duty to get ready to defend it when the time came. And once he became a soldier he found that he enjoyed the life very much, and for eleven years he had a wild time and did many evil things for which afterwards he was very sorry.

In the year 1508 he was sent in command of a company of soldiers to defend the fortress of Castelnuovo, not far from Treviso, against the attacking Germans. He found the castle in a bad state. The walls were crumbling away, and he did not see how he could hold it against the enemy. Although he and his men fought very bravely, they were easily overcome, and he found himself imprisoned in a deep dungeon, with fetters on his wrists, and his leg chained to a huge and heavy ball of stone.

As the days went by he had time to think of the bad things he had done in his life, and he grew more and more sorry for them. He started to say his prayers again, and he made a vow that if ever he got out of prison the first thing he would do would be to make a pilgrimage to a chapel at Treviso which was dedicated to the Blessed Virgin Mary.

No sooner had he made this promise to Our Lady than he noticed on the floor a small key. He did not remember having seen it before, and managed to pick it up. It was the key that unlocked his fetters. But, although he now had the key, he was chained so carefully that he still found it impossible to get altogether free. Then the same kind of miracle happened as had happened not long after the days when Jesus had lived on earth and Saint Peter had been released from prison by an angel. Jerome realised that someone-he thought it might be Our Lady herself-was standing by his side, helping him to shake off all his chains and leading him out of his prison, opening all the doors before him as they went.

As soon as he was safe in the countryside he went, as he had promised, straight to the chapel at Treviso and told every one what had happened; and shortly afterwards, when the war was over and he was made Keeper of Castelnuovo, the first thing he did was to send the fetters and chains and the great stone ball to the chapel at Treviso to hang from the roof, so that all men would be reminded of the miracle.

He did not stay long at Castelnuovo, because his nephews in Venice needed him there to look after their education, and he himself wished to become a priest. In Venice he realised how many orphans there were who had no one to look after them and take an interest in their lives, and after a great plague and famine which swept over the land in the year 1528 there seemed to be more helpless and

The Saints

Level 4 - Lesson 8

unfortunate boys and girls without a home than ever. So, with one or two friends, he took a house near the Church of Saint Rose and turned it into a home for homeless children.
Gradually other people came to help him, and he founded a new Order, whose chief work was to look after orphans and the poor and the sick everywhere. The head quarters of this society was in a tiny village called Somascha, not far from the city of Milan, and so the Order became known as the Somaschans.

Jerome himself never stopped doing good works, and it was while he was nursing people who had an infectious disease that he caught it and died. But in Venice people always remembered the Saint, who became the 'Knight of Our Lady' when the orphans to whom he and his followers had given a home dressed themselves in white in her honour and went through the streets and squares of Venice singing her hymns. **His Feast Day is July 20th.**

Question 9 ◆ What type of life did Saint Jerome live whilst in the army?
Question 10 ◆ What caused Saint Jerome to change his life?
Question 11 ◆ How did Saint Jerome escape from prison?

Devotions

The Story of Fatima (continued)

The Mayor of the district kidnapped the children so they could not go to see Our Lady on the 13th of August. There were big crowds beginning to gather on the day of the expected apparitions, and he wanted the people to think that the children were making up the stories about the Lady. Although the children were unable to be at the Cova on the 13th, Our Lady did appear to them when they returned from gaol on the 19th.

On the 13th of September, the big crowd said the Rosary with the children. The Lady's message this time was, Continue to say the Rosary in order to end the war. In October Our Lord will come, and Our Lady of Sorrows and Our Lady of Mount Carmel. Saint Joseph will appear with the Child Jesus to bless the world.

The big day finally came – 13th October, 1917. Although there was torrential rain a huge crowd of people, estimated to be over 70,000 came, they knelt in the mud and humbly prayed the Rosary with the children. Everything happened as Our Blessed Lady predicted with the great miracle of the gyrating of the sun towards the earth and then its return to the sky. There were also the apparitions as Our Lady had promised, that only the children saw.

Another miracle: the sun shone after it was back on course, and the crowd found that their formally sodden clothes were dry and comfortable again, without trace of mud or rain.

That day, thousands of people left Fatima knowing that heaven had visited earth.

Question 12   ◆   How many people witnessed the Miracle of the sun?
Question 13   ◆   Why did the children not attend the apparition on August 13th?
Question 14   ◆   What was Our Lady's main message to the children in September?

General

The Seven Steps to the Priesthood

When a young man wishes to become a priest, he must first of all be accepted into a Seminary (or Monastery). After a short time he is tonsured; that is, he becomes a cleric. A cleric is a person who is dedicating his life to God and is training to be a priest or is a priest. The remainder of us are laymen. Once a man has been tonsured, he has many years of study and training to undergo before he is ordained a priest. In fact, he has seven steps to take before becoming a priest, seven ordinations on the way. In this lesson, we will learn the names of the steps and very briefly, a little about each step.

The first four steps are called the minor orders and the last three steps are called the major orders.

Minor Orders:

1. **Porter** : holds the key to the Church and has the responsibility of determining who can and cannot enter God's House.
2. **Lector** : is able to read or sing the epistle during Mass
3. **Exorcist** : has the power to bless food and to expel the devil
4. **Acolyte** : carries the candles at holy Mass (this minor order is usually done by altar boys today, but it is a privilege, not a right)

Major Orders:

5. **Sub deacon** : assists the priest at a High Mass
6. **Deacon** : can read or sing the gospel, can distribute Holy Communion, can baptise, can give the sermon at Mass.
7. **Priest** : has the power to forgive sins and to consecrate the Body and Blood of Our Lord.

Question 15 ◆ List, in order, the seven steps to the priesthood.
Question 16 ◆ How many minor orders are there?
Question 17 ◆ What powers/rights are given to a deacon?
Question 18 ◆ What do we mean when we say the Church is One?

Lesson 9

Level 4

Pre - Confirmation

Catechism

The Seventh Commandment

115. What is the seventh commandment?

The seventh commandment of God is: Thou shalt not steal.

116. What are we commanded by the seventh commandment?

By the seventh commandment we are commanded to respect what belongs to others.

117. What does the seventh commandment forbid?

The seventh commandment forbids all dishonesty, such as stealing, cheating, unjust keeping of what belongs to others, and unjust damage to the property of others.

118. Are we obliged to restore to the owner stolen goods, or their value?

We are obliged to restore to the owner stolen goods, or their value, whenever we are able.

The seventh commandment forbids us from stealing, but also it obliges us to pay back anything we have taken. It is not sufficient to tell the priest in confession that we have stolen some money and that we are sorry if we will not return the money, or if we have spent it with no intention of returning it to its owner. This is a very important aspect of the seventh commandment of which many children (and alas, some adults) are not aware.

Question 1	◆	What does the seventh commandment forbid?
Question 2	◆	Are we obliged to restore to the owner stolen goods, or their value?
Question 3	◆	What does the sixth commandment forbid?

Level 4 - Lesson 9

Prayer

The Morning Offering

Each morning, upon rising we should say a good Morning Offering. There are many versions and it does not matter which one you say; they are all similar. In the next few lessons we will study the Morning Offering; the prayer which begins each of the days God has given us.

Oh my Jesus, through the most pure Heart of Mary

Whenever we pray to Jesus, we go through Mary. Many non Catholics cannot understand this and even call it evil. How far from the truth is this! In the gospel, it tells us that the three Wise Men were looking for Jesus and they found Him with His Mother Mary. When you find Mary, you find Jesus. God Himself wills that we pray through His most holy Mother. Thus, the first prayer we pray each day, addressed to Our Divine Lord, is through His Mother and our Mother. And we remind ourselves each time we say these words that Our Lady is Immaculate – pure.

Question 4 ◆ Give two reasons why we pray through Mary.
Question 5 ◆ What is another word for pure?
Question 6 ◆ What petition are we asking of Our Blessed Mother in the Hail Mary?

Bible Story

Jesus is Nailed to the Cross and Dies

When they arrived at Calvary, the cross was put on the ground, and the soldiers took Jesus and stripped off his clothes. Then Jesus was laid upon the cross, and men came with a hammer and nails. They roughly pulled our Saviour's hand to one side of the cross, and drove the large nail through it, fastening it to the cross; they did the same with the other hand. The feet were then nailed to the hard wood, and so Jesus was fastened to the cross. The nails were large, to bear the weight. What pain it must have been! Fancy each blow of the hammer driving the nail through the flesh! How sick Mary must have felt at the dreadful sound of the hammer! We cannot even imagine the pain of Jesus. We would scream and cry out if a pin were put through our hand; but Jesus was quite silent.

On the Cross

Have you seen men put a large stone, or pillar, or pole into the ground? They first dig a deep hole, then they tie ropes to the pole, and place one end of the pole just by the hole. Then they go a good many feet off and pull on these ropes. The pole slowly rises up, and goes into the hole with a sudden jerk. That is how the cross on which Jesus was nailed was jerked into the hole. That jerk must have been a terrible agony. The wounds in the hands and feet must have been torn larger by it, and must have bled more. At the foot of the cross stood Mary and John. You remember that Simeon had told Mary, long ago, that a sword of sorrow should pierce her heart; and what sorrow could be greater than to see a good, tender Son suffer such pain at the hands of cruel men? When Jesus was hanging there in this cruel state, the Jews mocked Him, saying: "He saved others: let Him save Himself, if He be Christ." And the soldiers also mocked Him, saying: "If Thou be the King of the Jews, save Thyself;" and Pilate had written on the top of His cross, in scorn, these words: Jesus of Nazareth, King of the Jews. That is what the "I.N.R.I." means on the crucifixes you see. But Jesus still loved and prayed for His persecutors, saying: "Father, forgive them, for they know not what they do."

The Thieves

The two bad men, who were thieves, or robbers, were also crucified with Jesus, being put at each side of Him. One of these robbers mocked Jesus, too, saying: "If Thou be Christ, save Thyself and us." But the other robber said to him in rebuke: "We suffer justly, for we received the due reward of our deeds; but this man hath done no evil." And he said to Jesus: "Lord, remember me when You come to Your kingdom." And Jesus said to him: "Amen, I say to thee, this day thou shalt be with Me in paradise."

Level 4 - Lesson 9

Bible Story

Jesus Speaks to Mary

When Jesus saw Mary standing with John at the foot of His cross, He said to Mary: "Woman, behold thy son," and to John: "Behold thy Mother." And from that hour the disciple took her as his own Mother.

Jesus Dies

Jesus had now been hanging in torture on the cross for three hours. He was in such pain of body and soul, that He called out: "My God, my God, why hast Thou forsaken Me?" He then said: "I thirst." A soldier who was near dipped a sponge in vinegar, and putting it on a spear, lifted it up to Jesus, who, when He had moistened His lips, cried out with a loud voice: "It is consummated," and then with a great cry of prayer: "Father, into Thy hands I commend My Spirit," He bowed His head and died. The soldiers were filled with fear, and cried out: "Indeed, this was the Son of God" – for the earth trembled, the rocks split, the sun was darkened, the graves opened, and the dead arose. The people went back to Jerusalem full of fear. Later a soldier opened the side of Jesus with a spear, and blood and water came out of the wound.

Question 7	◆	What does I.N.R.I. stand for?
Question 8	◆	What did Jesus say to the good thief?
Question 9	◆	What did Jesus mean when He said to Saint John, "Behold thy Mother"?

The Saints

Saint Thomas More

While in Italy, Saint Jerome Emiliani was fighting in the wars, there had come to the throne of England King Henry VIII. Henry VIII, like Henry II, had made one of his friends, called Thomas, the Chancellor of England, and hoped he would always do as the King wanted. His name was Thomas More. Besides being a very clever lawyer, he wrote books, and was a happy and amusing man, and the King liked to go down to Chelsea and visit him at his house there.

On one of these visits the King and Thomas walked chatting in the garden for more than an hour, and they seemed such good friends that afterwards More's son-in-law, William Roper, said to him, "You are indeed a fortunate man. The King had his arm round your shoulder as if you were his dearest friend."

"You are right, son Roper," said More, who knew that Henry really cared for no one but himself, "I think the King is as friendly to me as he is to any man in England. But that is nothing to be proud of, for I am sure that, if by having my head cut off he could win a castle in France, my head would go.

About this time the King got tired of his wife and wanted to get rid of her and marry some one else. When the Pope told him that he could not do such a thing, he decided that he would pay no attention to the Pope, but would get his own bishops to do what he wanted in England. So he had himself proclaimed Head of the Church of England, and made people take an oath that he and not the Pope was the person who could say what it was right to do. If they would not do this he had them put in prison and then killed.

A great many people in the Church saw no harm in this, but others said that no one but the successor of Saint Peter-the Pope-could be called Head of the Church, and they were ready to die rather than take the oath. Everybody thought that Thomas More would take it. He was not a priest or a bishop. He had a happy family whom he loved very dearly, as they loved him-especially his daughter Margaret, who was married to William Roper-and they and his other friends would say that, when so many bishops were taking the oath, there could be nothing wrong in it for him. But he knew there was. He said that it was as impossible for the Church in England to make its own particular laws which the rest of the Church did not agree with as it would be for the City of London to make one of its rules an Act of Parliament which should be lawful for the whole country.

When the day came for him to appear for trial he was at home with his family. He had to go to Lambeth Palace, which was the opposite side of the river Thames from his house, and as he went down to the riverside to take a boat he would not allow them to come with him, as they usually did, to say good-bye to him there. He was afraid that, because he loved them so much and did not want to leave them, he would become weak and take the oath after all.

So he took with him only his son-in-law William Roper and four servants, and got in the boat to row across the river. He was sad and troubled, and still had not quite made up his mind what to say at Lambeth. Then, just before they got to the landing-steps, he whispered to Roper, "Son Roper, I thank Our Lord the field is won."

He was sent to the Tower of London, brought out again for a public trial, and condemned to death. On his way back to the Tower for execution his daughter Margaret suddenly broke through the guards who were taking him there, and the crowd standing round, and, "openly in the sight of them all," threw her arm round his neck and kissed him.

Five days afterwards he was beheaded on Tower Hill. As he was going to the scaffold a man who in the old days had found comfort and wisdom in the advice of Thomas called out, "Mr More, do you know me? I am as troubled as ever I was."

More answered, "I remember you very well. Go your way in peace and pray for me; and I will not fail to pray for you."

More made a very short speech to the people who had come to see him die. There was much that he could have said, but the King had sent a message asking him to say little, and Thomas More, like Thomas of Canterbury, Hugh of Lincoln, and all the statesmen-saints, always obeyed the King in things that the King had a right to ask. He ended his short speech by saying, "I die the King's faithful servant, but God's first."

They set up his head on a pole over London Bridge, so that all people should see that even a great man who was the King's friend was shown no mercy when he refused to put the King's wishes before everything else. But one morning the head was not there. In the night his daughter Margaret, with trusty friends to help her, had stolen it to keep it safe and hidden until she herself died, when it was buried with her-the relic of her beloved father who was also a saint. **His feast day is July 9th.**

Question 10 ◆ What high position did Saint Thomas More hold?
Question 11 ◆ Why was Saint Thomas More put to death?
Question 12 ◆ How did Saint Jerome escape from prison?

Devotions

The Story of Fatima (continued)

We have read how the three children, Lucia, Francisco and Jacinta were visited by an angel in 1916 to prepare them for Our Lady's visit the following year. The joy they experienced during these apparitions was matched by the sufferings they endured by the disbelief of the authorities, Lucia's mother and the priest himself. They were even jailed for a short time.

During one of the apparitions, Our Lady told Francisco and Jacinta that they would die and go to heaven soon, but Lucia would have to stay behind for some time longer. Well, the two younger children, Francisco and Jacinta did die soon afterwards and Lucia, who is a Carmelite lived for a long time after and died in 2005.

Our Lady of Fatima has a message for us all. She wants us to change our lives, by praying the Rosary every day, by making sacrifices for poor sinners, by making reparation for our sins, by praying for the Pope and the clergy, by praying for the holy souls in purgatory, and by praying for the conversion of Russia. Could you imagine if every Catholic did all these things? What a wonderful world we would live in! And there is no reason why you can't do all these things.

Question 13 ◆ Which two children died soon after the apparitions?
Question 14 ◆ List three things Our Lady wants us to do to change our lives.
Question 15 ◆ Why did the children not attend the apparition on August 13th?

Level 4 - Lesson 9

General

We are not going to learn anything new in this lesson, but it is a good opportunity to revise all our work from the General Section studied this year.

Question 16 ◆ Who are bound to fast?
Question 17 ◆ How long is the fast before Holy Communion?
Question 18 ◆ What are the four divisions of Feast Days?
Question 19 ◆ What are the six seasons of the Church (in order)?
Question 20 ◆ How many chief Commandments of the Church are there?

Lesson 10

Level 4

Pre - Confirmation

Catechism

119. What is the eighth commandment of God?

The eighth commandment of God is: Thou shalt not bear false witness against thy neighbour.

120. What are we commanded by the eighth commandment?

By the eighth commandment we are commanded to speak the truth in all things.

121. What does the eighth commandment forbid?

The eighth commandment forbids lies and harming the name of another.

The eighth commandment teaches us to tell the truth always. Never to lie! There is no such thing as a small lie or a white lie. Any lie is an offence against God. We may never even tell a lie to gain some good. Why? Because every lie is a sin and offends God.

This commandment particularly teaches us not to gossip and talk about other people; certainly never to speak about untrue things, but even not to talk about our neighbour's faults unless it is absolutely necessary. It is not just children who find this commandment a difficult one, but many adults.

Question 1 ◆ What are we commanded by the eighth commandment?
Question 2 ◆ What does the eighth commandment forbid?
Question 3 ◆ Are we obliged to restore to the owner stolen goods, or their value?

Level 4 - Lesson 10

Prayer

The Morning Offering (continued)

I offer you my prayers, works, joys and sufferings of this day,

When we pray our Morning Offering, we offer everything we do during the day. It is almost impossible for a person to be thinking actively of God every second of the day. Therefore, we cannot always think to offer up everything we do. So, we offer it up every morning. If we do this, every single action and thought of ours becomes a prayer. We should never miss our Morning Offering. It is perhaps the most important prayer of the day.

For all the intentions of Thy Divine Heart.

We do not need to always list our intentions before God; He already knows them. When saying our Morning Offering, we are saying to Jesus, "Lord, take everything I have to offer today and use them as You wish". God rewards a generous soul and He will answer all our prayers and look after all our needs.

Amen. So be it

Question 4 ◆ Why is a Morning Offering necessary?
Question 5 ◆ Why do we not need to always list our intentions?
Question 6 ◆ Give two reasons why we pray through Mary.

Bible Story

Jesus in The Tomb – The Resurrection

Joseph of Arimathea, a rich man, and a ruler, who believed in secret in Jesus, went at night to Pilate, and asked leave to take the body of Jesus and bury it. Pilate gave leave. So Joseph and his friends took down the body of Jesus from the cross, and wrapped it in white cloths and sweet spices, and put it in the tomb. The tomb was a new one, and cut in a rock, and had a great stone to close it up. Joseph had intended it for his own body when he died. The rulers knew that Jesus had said He would rise again from the dead in three days, so they sent a guard of soldiers to watch the tomb, for they said the disciples will steal away the body, and say He has risen, and so people will believe. So Pilate put his great seal on the tomb.

The Resurrection

The third day had now come. It was the early morning, and the soldiers were at watch, when all at once the earth shook, and an angel came to the tomb and rolled back the stone. Jesus had risen, all glorious and beautiful. His face shone like the sun. The soldiers frightened by the earthquake and the shining brightness of the angel ran away and told the rulers. The rulers, who were now afraid that the Jews would believe, gave the soldiers a great sum of money, and told them to tell the Jews that the disciples had stolen the body. This the Jews believed.

Mary Magdalen and other women came that same morning to the tomb with spices. On their way, they asked one another how they should roll away the large stone from the entrance of the tomb, to anoint the Body. But when they arrived they found the stone removed, and the body of Jesus gone. Mary Magdalen left at once to tell the Apostles that the body of Jesus was gone. The other women looked into the tomb, for they saw a bright light, and there sat an angel, who said to them: "Be not afraid: you seek Jesus of Nazareth, who was crucified: He is risen; He is not here, behold the place where they laid Him. But go tell His disciples and Peter, that He goeth before you into Galilee; there you shall see Him, as He told you." But the women ran away in fright, and told no one.

Question 7	◆	In whose tomb was Our Lord placed?
Question 8	◆	Why did the Jews believe that the Body of Jesus had been stolen?
Question 9	◆	For how many days was Jesus in the tomb?
Question 10	◆	What does I.N.R.I. stand for?

The Saints

Saint Boniface

Saint Boniface, who is known as 'the Apostle of Germany,' was born at Crediton, in Devonshire, about 680, while St Giles was alive. His English name was Winfred, and he was five when he was sent to school at the Benedictine monastery at Exeter. It was just at that time that all England finally became Christian, and as Winfred grew up he was determined to become a missionary to Germany, the land of his ancestors, where the old gods, Odin and Thor, were still worshiped.

But before he could do this there was much learning to be done. He was made a monk, was made head of an abbey school not far from Winchester, which was then the capital of England, and when he was thirty-six he set sail on his first mission with three companions in a German trading-vessel which he found on a visit to the little port of London.

He travelled across the North Sea, with these companions and their soldier-leader, Charles Martel, who was a Christian. Saint Boniface soon found that as long as the Christian Charles Martel was striking down the German pagans with his battleaxe they were not going to pay any attention to him, a poor wandering monk, who was telling them that they must give up their warlike ways and bow down to the Cross of Christ. So he returned to England to think out the best way to deal with the situation.

The next time he set out it was not to Germany he went but to Rome, to put the matter before the Pope and ask him what he should do. The Pope sent him to Germany again, as he asked to be sent, to make a report on the country and to see how it could best be made Christian. Boniface crossed the Alps and so came first to the south of Germany-to Bavaria and, going northward, to Thuringia, where once Christianity had been known-and by the time that he arrived back in Friesland, on the borders of the North Sea, everything had changed. Charles Martel had won his battles, the pagan duke of the Frisians was dead, and Christianity was already proclaimed the religion of the land. In those days a country had the same religion as its ruler, and as Charles Martel was a Christian, the Frisians were called Christians.

But really the people secretly, and in many places openly, still worshiped the old gods. Boniface sent for helpers from among his friends in England, and they went about the country founding monasteries and nunaries which should be centres of teaching for the pagans round about. The Pope made him the first 'Bishop of All Germany,' and Charles Martel saw to it that he was protected. For, as Boniface explained to his friend the Bishop of Winchester, without Charles' help he could neither defend his monks nor prevent idolatry. But he himself went about all the time, risking his own life to preach the Gospel and to try to make the Germans Christian at heart.

One of the sacred places of the heathen Germans was near Geismar, where there was an enormous oak-tree called 'Thor's Oak.' Boniface called together all the people of the neighborhood who he knew still met there in the dead of night to worship Thor. Then when they were assembled-"a great crowd of pagans bitterly cursing in their hearts this enemy of their gods," as the old chronicler describes them-Boniface took an axe and cut a notch at the base of the tree, calling on them to watch how little sacred the oak was. But when he had made a superficial cut, suddenly the oak's vast bulk shaken by a mighty blast of wind, crashed to the ground, shivering its topmost branches into fragments in its fall; as if by the express will of God, for the monks present had done nothing

The Saints

to cause it. Many of the heathens there who had expected Thor to strike Boniface dead with a thunderbolt were converted on the spot and helped Boniface and the monks to build, from the timber of the oak, a little chapel which was dedicated to Saint Peter.

Boniface continued his work of conversion till he was over seventy, when at last he was martyred by an armed band of still heathen Germans on the borders of Friesland. He had appointed a day when all those who had recently been baptised should come together so that he, as their Bishop, could confirm them. No sooner had they gathered than a great number of pagans, armed with spears and shields, rushed upon them. Boniface's attendants wanted to stand and fight, but he, perhaps remembering those long-ago days when fighting had prevented him making any converts, said: "Lay down your arms, for we are told in Scripture not to render evil for evil but to overcome evil by good. Endure with steadfast mind the sudden onslaught of death that you may be able to reign evermore with Christ." While he was speaking the enemy rushed on the Christians and killed them. When, after they had gone, Boniface's body was found he was still holding the book he had been reading – Saint Ambrose's 'How to die well'.

Boniface was first buried in his cathedral at Mainz, but later men remembered that when he was alive he had said he wished to be buried in the Abbey of Fulda, which he had built at the beginning of his missionary work, so they reburied the body there. Saint Boniface's Feast Day is June 5th.

Question 11   What title did the Pope give to Saint Boniface?
Question 12   ◆   Who protected Saint Boniface?
Question 13   ◆   How did Saint Boniface die?
Question 14   ◆   What high position did Saint Thomas More hold?
              ◆

Devotions

Fatima – The First Saturdays

Our Lady appeared to the little shepherds again at other times, although not in the Cova da Iria. A short time before the death of Francisco, when he and his sister Jacinta were very ill, she came to tell them that She would soon come to fetch them to Heaven. Francisco was the first to go – it was the 4th of April, 1919, Jacinta was to go to two hospitals, "not to be cured, but to suffer more for the conversion of sinners."
Near the end Our Lady appeared to her and said these grave words to her, which are also directed to us: She told her "that the sin which sends most people to perdition is the sin of the flesh; that they should do without luxuries; that people should not remain obstinate in their sins as they had done up to then; that it was necessary to do much penance." On saying this, Our Lady was very sad. Because of this, Jacinta often exclaimed: "Oh, I am so sorry for Our Lady! I am so sorry for her!" On the 20th of February, 1920, Our Lady fulfilled Her promise to take the second of Her little shepherds "soon" to Heaven. But Divine Providence had not yet finished the work resolved upon in regard to Fatima, and so Lucia, the oldest of the three little ones, was told that "she would stay here some time longer." Our Lady said to her that "in order to prevent the war She would come to ask for the Consecration of Russia to Her Immaculate Heart and the Communion of Reparation on the first Saturdays." This She did on the 10th of December, 1925, and in June 1929, in Pontevedra and Tuy where Sister Lucia then was, at the time, a Dorothean Religious.
On the 10th of December, 1925, the Most Holy Virgin Mary appeared to Lucia, with the Child Jesus by Her side, elevated on a cloud of light. Our Lady rested one hand on Lucia's shoulder, while in the other hand She held a heart surrounded with sharp thorns. At the same time the Child Jesus spoke: "Have pity on the Heart of your Most Holy Mother. It is covered with the thorns with which ungrateful men pierce it at every moment, and there is no one to remove them with an act of reparation.
Then Our Lady said to Lucia: "My daughter, look at My Heart surrounded with the thorns with which ungrateful men pierce it at every moment by their blasphemies and ingratitude. You, at least, try to console me, and say that I promise to assist at the hour of death with all the graces necessary for salvation all those who, on the first Saturday of five consecutive months, go to Confession and receive Holy Communion, recite five decades of the Rosary and keep me company for a quarter of an hour while meditating on the mysteries of the Rosary, with the intention of making reparation to me."
On the 15th of February, 1926, the Child Jesus again appeared to Lucia, asking her if she had spread this devotion of reparation to the Immaculate Heart of His Holy Mother. Lucia told Him of the difficulties pointed out by her confessor, and though the Mother Superior ardently desired to propagate the devotion, her confessor also warned her that she could do nothing by herself alone. Our Lord replied: "It is true that your superior alone can do nothing, but with My grace she can do all."
Lucia then spoke of the difficulty which some people had of confessing on Saturday, and asked if Confession within eight days would be valid. Jesus replied: "Yes, even more time still, as long as they receive Me in the state of grace and have the intention of making reparation to the Immaculate Heart of Mary." She asked: "My Jesus, what about those who forget to make this intention?" Jesus replied: "They can do so at their next confession, taking advantage of their first opportunity to go to Confession."
Oh what love Jesus and Mary have for us! This wonderful devotion of the First Five Saturdays is a real opportunity for us to be always prepared for heaven. We should never be satisfied with Purgatory; it is a state, full of suffering and it does not please Our Lord if we are not striving to do all for Him.

Question 15 ◆ Summarize what is necessary to make the First Five Saturdays.

Level 4 - Lesson 10

General

Catholic Etiquette

We spend much time learning our faith; our catechism, lives of the Saints, the Bible etc., but we sometimes neglect something most obvious – the day to day way of living as a child of God. We are going to study things which may seem obvious, but which are so very important; Catholic etiquette or Catholic courtesy or simply, Catholic manners.

Catholic children (and adults) must be different than all others. We should not hide the fact that we are Catholic. That does not mean that we 'show off', but it does mean that we should not be afraid to do the normal things that a Catholic should do every day, e.g. when at a restaurant, saying our grace before and after meals, including making a Sign of the Cross. We should have no regard for what others think of us, that is, we should have no human respect.

When writing letters, we should always write in a Catholic manner; never writing badly of others, or gossiping. A very good habit is to write something at the top of each page (this could also be done on pages of your school work, as it is on every page of these lessons), such as JMJ, which means, Jesus, Mary and Joseph, or AMDG which stands for Ad Majorem Dei Gloriam meaning, all for the greater glory of God, or even by placing a simple cross at the top of each page. These things are a constant reminder to us, and others, that all we do is offered up to God. It is living our Morning Offering throughout the day.

Another good habit is to write SAG on the back of the envelope when we send a letter. This means, Saint Anthony Guide, and once again, it is a prayer and a little sign that your faith is living and is not restricted to one hour on a Sunday morning.

There are many other such things that can be done, and it is good to start these little practices, for they lead us to God

Control your tongue. Do not say anything contrary to charity, modesty, or good manners.

Question 16 ◆ What is another name for Catholic Etiquette?
Question 17 ◆ What do we mean by human respect?

Lesson 11

Level 4

Pre - Confirmation

Catechism

The Ninth and Tenth Commandment

122. **What is the ninth commandment of God?**

The ninth commandment of God is: Thou shalt not covet thy neighbour's wife.

123. **What are we commanded by the ninth commandment?**

By the ninth commandment we are commanded to be pure in thought and in desire.

124. **What is forbidden by the ninth commandment?**

The ninth commandment forbids all thoughts and desires contrary to chastity.

125. **What is the tenth commandment of God?**

The tenth commandment of God is: Thou shalt not covet thy neighbour's goods.

126. **What does the tenth commandment forbid?**

The tenth commandment forbids all desire to take or to keep unjustly what belongs to others, and also forbids envy at their success.

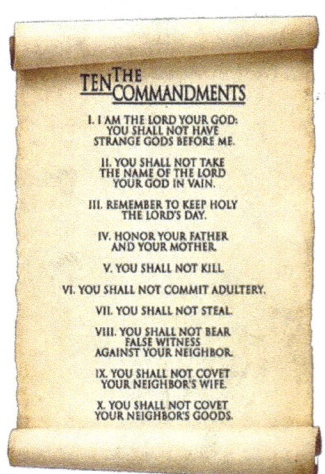

The ninth and tenth commandments command and forbid that same things as the sixth and seventh commandments (respectively) command and forbid, with the exception they forbid thoughts and desires, whereas the sixth and seventh commandments forbid the acts themselves. Therefore, to steal from a bank is breaking the seventh commandment, but the desire to take money is breaking the tenth commandment.

Question 1 ◆ What is forbidden by the ninth commandment?
Question 2 ◆ What does the tenth commandment forbid?
Question 3 ◆ What are we commanded by the eighth commandment?

Level 4 - Lesson 11

Prayer

The Act of Contrition

Each night, before we go to bed, we should kneel down, say our night prayers and our Act of Contrition. Each time we go to Confession, we also say an Act of Contrition. But do we really understand what we are saying? To make a perfect Act of Contrition we must understand what we are saying, otherwise, are we truly sorry for offending Our Lord? We are going to study in detail what this prayer really means, so that each time we pray it, we will profit by it.

O my God I am sorry and beg pardon for all my sins

We address the Blessed Trinity in this prayer. We pray to the Three Divine Persons, the Father, Son and Holy Ghost. We tell God that we are sorry for all our sins and that we ask His forgiveness. We should only say this prayer if we are truly sorry for our sins.

I detest them above all things

What we are really saying here is that sin is repulsive to us. We are telling God that we would rather be stricken with blindness or another disease, rather than to commit one sin. These are strong words we are praying.

Because they deserve Thy dreadful punishments

When we sin, especially when we sin mortally, we are rightly worried about the consequences of what we have done. Our Lord told us that if we die in the state of mortal sin, we will spend our eternity in the fires of hell. That is frightening indeed! So we are telling God that we are sorry because we do not want to suffer the fires of hell. This is called imperfect contrition. It is enough to have our mortal sins forgiven in Confession.

Question 4	◆	What is the first reason that we are sorry for our sins in the Act of Contrition?
Question 5	◆	Whom do we address when we pray the Act of Contrition?
Question 6	◆	Why is a Morning Offering necessary?

Bible Story

Jesus Appears to His Friends

Mary Magdalen ran and told Peter and the other disciple whom Jesus loved "They have taken away the Lord out of the sepulchre, and we know not where they have laid Him." Peter and John ran to the tomb, but they could find no body, and returned to their homes. Mary stayed at the tomb weeping, and stooping down looking in the tomb, she saw two angels in white, and they said to her: "Woman, why weepest thou?" She said to them: "Because they have taken away my Lord, and I know not where they have laid Him." When she turned round she saw a man standing, who she thought was the gardener, and she said to Him: "Sir, if thou hast taken Him hence, tell me where thou hast laid Him, and I will take Him away." Jesus (for it was Jesus) said to her: "Mary." She turning, said to Him "Rabboni" (Master). Jesus then told her to go and tell His apostles, and say to them: "I ascend to My Father and to your Father, to My God and your God;" and Mary did as she was told.

Jesus Appears to His Apostles

The apostles were that day in a room, with the door closed, afraid of the Jews, when Jesus came in, they knew not how, and said to them: "Peace be to you;" and when He had said this, He showed them His hands and His side and they were glad to see Him. Thomas, who was one of the disciples, was not present when Jesus was there, and on his return the other disciples said to him: "We have seen the Lord." But he said to them: "Except I shall see in His hands the print of the nails, and put my finger into the place of the nails, and put my hand into His side, I will not believe." When eight days were passed, the disciples were again in the same room, and Thomas was with them. Jesus came, the doors being shut, and stood in the midst, and said: "Peace be to you." Then He said to Thomas: "Put in thy finger hither, and see My hands; and bring hither thy hand and put it into My side; and be not faithless, but believing." Thomas answered, and said to Him: "My Lord and my God." Jesus said to him: "Because thou hast seen Me, Thomas, thou hast believed; blessed are they that have not seen and have believed?

Question 7	◆	Who spoke to Mary Magdalen at the tomb?
Question 8	◆	Which one of the Apostles refused to believe that Jesus had risen unless he could see for Himself?
Question 9	◆	What did Jesus say to Saint Thomas after Saint Thomas said, "My Lord and my God"?
Question 10	◆	In whose tomb was Our Lord placed?

The Saints

Saint Peter Canisius

Just as Saint Boniface is known as 'the Apostle of Germany,' so Saint Peter Canisius, who was born in 1521, is called 'the Second Apostle of Germany.' At the time of his birth a German monk, Martin Luther, had broken away from the Catholic Church, and by his preaching had influenced many of the German princes to follow him and join his new 'Lutheran,' or 'Protestant,' Church. So, by the time that Peter Canisius had finished his studies at the University and had taken his degree of Master of Arts at Cologne, great parts of Germany were no longer Catholic.

This made Peter very sad, and when he heard that there was in the neighbourhood a member of the new Order of the Society of Jesus, which Saint Ignatius of Loyola had founded a few years earlier to fight for the faith, Peter set out to visit him. The result was that Peter Canisius himself joined the Society of Jesus and before long went to Rome to see Saint Ignatius himself. Many of the Jesuits were going as missionaries to far off lands, but Peter thought, and later said; that to defend the faith at home was just as important as to convert the Hindus, and he hoped that he would be allowed to go back and work in Germany.

Fortunately for him, at this time the Duke of Bavaria, who had remained faithful to the Church, was worried about what would happen to the University of Ingoldstadt and sent to Saint Ignatius for help. In the struggle between the Catholics and the Protestants, the universities, as centres of learning, were very important, and the Duke was anxious that Ingoldstadt should be in the hands of a good and fearless scholar. So Saint Ignatius decided to send Peter Canisius, with two others, to teach there.

Before he left Rome Peter went to pray at the tombs of Saints Peter and Paul, and he has left a record of what he felt as he was doing so:

> They gave me their blessing and strengthened me for my mission to Germany,
> and seemed to promise their assistance to me as an apostle to Germany.
> From that day forth Germany occupied more and more of my anxious thoughts,
> and I longed to spend myself utterly in life and death for her salvation.

Peter Canisius was only twenty-eight when he took up his work at Ingoldstadt, and he lived till he was seventy-six, spending all his time, not only at Ingoldstadt but later at many other places all over Germany where he was sent to preach and teach, in defending the Faith in learning and argument, with his tongue and with his pen.

He realised that one of the important things to be done was to see that people, young and old, knew the simple truths about the Catholic Faith; so he wrote a short catechism, in Latin and German, which before his death went into two hundred editions and was translated into twelve European languages. This short catechism was intended for children and was an extract from

The Saints

the great catechism he wrote for students at the universities, which contained 222 questions, 2000 quotations from the Bible, and 1200 from the Fathers of the Church among the answers. It was the model for all later catechisms, and even two hundred years later there were many places where the word 'Canisius' was used instead of the word 'catechism'.

Peter was one of the kindest and gentlest of men. He preferred just to state the truth and not to argue about it. He never lost his temper. When he first arrived at Ingoldstadt he found that the head of the school and library there was a disagreeable man who was spending the University's money on Lutheran books. Peter, though he could have done so, did not order him to change his ways, but instead performed so many acts of kindness, and said so many prayers for him, that in a very short time the man was overcome with shame, burnt the books he had bought, and mended his ways. Even the Protestants loved this 'Second Apostle of Germany' whom one of them described as "a noble Jesuit whose character no blemish stains." The feast of Saint Peter Canisius is April 27th.

St. Peter Canisius

Let my eyes take their sleep, but may my heart always keep watch for you.

Question 11 ◆ To what Order did Saint Peter Canisius belong?
Question 12 ◆ Why did Saint Peter Canisius want to be sent back to Germany to work, rather than in the mission fields?
Question 13 ◆ What title did the Pope give to Saint Boniface?

Devotions

Fatima – The Last Vision, The Consecration of Russia

In June, 1929, Our Lady appeared again to ask the Consecration of Russia to Her Immaculate Heart, "promising by this means to prevent the spreading of its errors and to bring about its conversion." But only on 20th December, 1940, eleven years later, was Lucia authorised to write to the Holy Father Pope Pius XII, asking this Consecration. This is how Lucia describes this apparition in a letter: "Suddenly the whole Chapel was illumined by a supernatural light, and a cross of light appeared above the altar, reaching to the ceiling. In a bright light at the upper part of the cross could be seen the face of a man and His body to the waist (Father), on his breast there was a dove also of light (Holy Ghost) and, nailed to the cross, was the body of another man (Son). Drops of blood were falling from the face of Jesus Crucified and from the wound in His side. These drops ran down on to the Host and fell into the chalice. Our Lady was beneath the right arm of the cross (..it was Our Lady of Fatima with Her Immaculate Heart…in Her left hand….without flames….).

Under the left arm of the cross, large letters, as of crystal clear water which ran down over the altar, formed these words: "Graces and Mercy". "I understood that it was the Mystery of the Most Holy Trinity which was shown to me, and I received lights about this Mystery which I am not permitted to reveal. "Our Lady then said to me: "The moment has come when God asks the Holy Father, in union with all the Bishops of the world, to make the Consecration of Russia to my Heart, promising to save it by this means."

Thus concludes the Story of Fatima; a story of the love that Mary has for this world. All we need to do is to obey her wishes and the world will be saved. If every child studying these lessons would do what Our Lady asked, we would please her very much and bring down God's mercy to this valley of tears.

Question 14 ◆ What did Our Lady ask for in this final vision?
Question 15 ◆ What Mystery was Lucia shown in this last vision?
Question 16 ◆ Summarise what is necessary to make the First Five Saturdays.

Level 4 - Lesson 11

General

Catholic Etiquette (continued)

In the last lesson you learnt about some Catholic practices when writing. In this lesson you are going to learn three Catholic practices which will help you to make your day more pleasing to God.

The first practice is whenever you pass a Catholic Church, make a Sign of the Cross out of respect for the Real Presence of Our Lord in the Church.

The second practice is similar. Whenever you pass a cemetery, say an Eternal Rest for the souls in that cemetery. These 'little things', done every day, not only increase your fervour as a Catholic, but are a reminder to the world which sees you, that Christ is indeed King of the world and we, His subjects.

The third practice is the blessing of the hours. This was a practice that the holy Cure of Ars promoted and practised. That is, at each new hour (e.g. eleven o'clock), you say a Hail Mary. This prayer need not be said aloud, but by saying it each and every hour, it keeps your mind firmly fixed on God and reminds you that God is giving you another hour of life to love and serve Him.

4 TIMES TO MAKE THE SIGN OF THE CROSS
(APART FROM YOUR TIME OF PRAYER)

WHEN PASSING BY A CHURCH
To honor the Blessed Sacrament present inside.

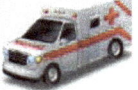
WHEN YOU HEAR A SIREN
To heal those in danger of dying.

WHEN PASSING BY A CEMETERY
As a prayer for the Holy Souls and those who have passed recently.

WHEN YOU SEE AN ACCIDENT
As a protection for those in peril.

YOU MAY ADD 1 OUR FATHER OR 1 HAIL MARY

Question 17	◆	What three practices have we studied this lesson?
Question 18	◆	Why should we make a Sign of the Cross when passing a Catholic Church?
Question 19	◆	What do we mean by human respect?

Lesson 12

Level 4

Pre - Confirmation

Catechism

The First Commandment of the Church

127. Which are the chief commandments, or laws, of the Church?

The chief commandments, or laws, of the Church are these six:

1) *To assist at Mass on all Sundays and holy days of obligation.*
2) *To fast and to abstain on the days appointed.*
3) *To confess our sins at least once a year.*
4) *To receive Holy Communion during the Easter time.*
5) *To contribute to the support of the Church.*
6) *To observe the laws of the Church concerning marriage.*

128. What sin does a Catholic commit who through his own fault misses Mass on a Sunday or holy day of obligation?

A Catholic who through his own fault misses Mass on a Sunday or holy day of obligation commits a mortal sin.

129. What else does the Church oblige us to do on holy days of obligation?

The Church obliges us to abstain from servile work on holy days of obligation, just as on Sundays, as far as we are able.

God has given us the Ten Commandments, which are the laws that govern all men in all times; they cannot change. God's Church too, has given us commandments which are also binding. The laws of the Church can change and have changed over the years. They are laws/commandments which help us to observe better the Ten Commandments.

Question 1	◆	What else does the Church oblige us to do on holy days of obligation?
Question 2	◆	Which are the chief commandments, or laws, of the Church?
Question 3	◆	What does the tenth commandment forbid?

Level 4 - Lesson 12

Prayer

The Act of Contrition (continued)

Because they have crucified my loving Saviour, Jesus Christ,

The second reason for our contrition (sorrow) is that we admit and acknowledge that it is our sins which have helped crucify our dear Saviour. This is a much more perfect contrition because we are not sorry because of the punishment due to us, but because we have hurt Our Lord.

And most of all because they offend Thine Infinite Goodness.

We are telling God with these words that the main cause of our sorrow is that we have offended God Himself; this God Who has given us everything, including life itself, we have offended Him. This is a perfect Act of Contrition.

Question 4 ◆ What is another word for contrition?
Question 5 ◆ Of the three reasons we are sorry for having offended God, which is the most perfect reason?
Question 6 ◆ Whom do we address when we pray the Act of Contrition?

Bible Story

Jesus Promises the Holy Ghost

Jesus had often shown Himself to His disciples, and on one occasion when He came to them He breathed on them, and said to them: "Receive ye the Holy Ghost, whose sins you shall forgive they are forgiven them, and whose sins you shall retain they are retained." Jesus in saying this, gave power to His apostles, and to His priests, to forgive our sins, if we confess them and are sorry for them. He taught them many things they had not known before. Forty days after Jesus had left the tomb and risen from the dead, He came again to the disciples, and told them to stay in Jerusalem for some days, for He was about to leave them, but would send the Holy Ghost to comfort them. He also told them to go into the whole world and preach the gospel to every creature.

Question 7 ♦ After the Resurrection, what did Jesus promise to His disciples?
Question 8 ♦ What power did Jesus give to His Apostles?
Question 9 ♦ Which one of the Apostles refused to believe that Jesus had risen unless he could see for himself?

Level 4 - Lesson 12

The Saints

Saint Germain

About four years after Saint Ambrose was made Archbishop, a boy named Germain was born in Auxerre to one of the noblest families in Gaul, which, like the rest of the Roman Empire, was then of course, Christian. After studying at the great schools of Arles and Lyons, he went to finish his education in Rome itself. Here he became a lawyer; and so clever and eloquent was he that the Emperor took notice of him and gave him one of the great ladies of the court, Eustachia, as his wife. Then he sent him back to Gaul as one of the six dukes who ruled the country for Rome.

Germain, Duke of Burgundy, went to live in his own town of Auxerre, and held there a magnificent court. Rich and important, he enjoyed himself as much as he could, and, though he was a baptised Christian, did not take his faith very seriously. His favourite sport was hunting, and he used to hang the trophies of the chase on one particular tree which in the old pagan days had been a sacred place.

Amator, the Bishop of Auxerre, went to him again and again, and asked him not to do this because it made some of the simple people who still did not quite understand Christianity think there was not much difference between it and the worship of the old gods. But Germain would not listen to him; and at last one day, when Germain was away in another part of the country, Amator had the tree cut down and burnt all the heads and antlers of the beasts which hung on it.

When the Duke came back and found what the Bishop had done he was so angry that he threatened to kill Amator, and actually set off with some of his soldiers to drag him from the church. But Amator did one of the strangest things that any bishop has ever done – though he had got permission from his superiors to do it while Germain was still away. Germain had come to use force on Amator; but once inside the church it was Amator who used force on Germain. The Bishop ordered the doors of the church to be barred against the Duke's attendants and then, against Germain's will, laid hands on him and ordained him a deacon. "Now you must live," he said, "as one who will be Bishop of Auxerre when I am dead."

Germain came out of the church a changed man. He was no longer angry, but accepted what had been done as the will of God. He gave himself up to prayer and good works, he gave away his great wealth to the poor and needy; and when, a very short time afterwards, Amator died, he became his successor. The proud Duke of Burgundy had become the humble Bishop of Auxerre.

The Saints

About ten years later the Church in Britain was in great difficulties. A clever man named Pelagius was preaching something which was not Christian doctrine, but which he pretended was the Faith; and many Christians were following him in his heresy – as this kind of false teaching is called. The Christians who remained faithful sent to the Pope to ask him for some one to help them in arguments against the doctrines of Pelagius. Who was better fitted than Germain, brilliant lawyer and faithful Christian? So Germain, with some companions, crossed to Britain and in a great argument with the heretics at St Alban's showed how wrong Pelagius was.

Germain stayed for some time in Britain, where later he helped the Britons in a very different way – which was a reminder that he had not only been a lawyer but a duke. At this time the Roman garrisons had been withdrawn from Britain, and the fierce Saxon invaders, helped by the Picts from beyond the North Wall, were attacking the British army. Germain suggested to the Britons that as the Saxons and the Picts advanced to give battle they should pray and then give three times the Easter cry: Alleluia! The army did so, and at the sound the enemy fled. Germain's advice had won for the Britons what is known in history as the "Alleluia victory."

When Germain got back to Gaul he found that the people of Brittany had been in rebellion, and he promised to put their case to the Emperor and to ask mercy for them. It was while in Italy on this mission that he died; but, as he had asked, the rebels were forgiven. And, as he asked, too, his body was sent back to be buried at his home, Auxerre. Saint Germain's feast day is July 31st.

Question 10 ♦ What did the Bishop of Auxerre do, which converted Germain?
Question 11 ♦ Against whose false teaching did Saint Germain preach?
Question 12 ♦ Why did Saint Peter Canisius want to be sent back to Germany to work, rather than in the mission fields?

Devotions

Devotion to the Sacred Heart of Jesus
The Nine First Fridays

We are going to learn about the apparitions of Jesus to Saint Margaret Mary and the beginning of what we call the Nine First Fridays' Devotions.
It was just as Jansenism was causing a "coldness" to enter into Catholic life in France, that the revelations to Saint Margaret Mary Alacoque, concerning devotion to the Sacred Heart of Jesus, were made.

This was a devotion in which the heart symbolised Jesus' perfect love for mankind. The first apparition took place on the 27th of December, the feast of Saint John the Evangelist, in 1673, while Saint Margaret Mary was a nun in the Visitation convent at Paray-le-Monial. She related what happened to Father Claude de la Colombiere, who was in charge of the Jesuit house in the town, describing how she had a vision of Jesus, during which she was given some idea of the greatness of His love for mankind. Jesus told her that He wanted her to tell the people of this love, and a similar theme was expressed during the second apparition, early in 1674, when Saint Margaret Mary saw Jesus' Sacred Heart on a throne of flames, transparent as crystal, surrounded by a crown of thorns signifying the sins of mankind, with a cross above it.

Again Jesus told her of His infinite love for mankind and His desire that He should be honoured through the display of this image of His Heart, with the promise that all who did so would be specially blessed.

Question 13 ◆ To whom did Jesus reveal the Devotion of the Nine First Fridays?
Question 14 ◆ What does the Sacred Heart represent? (symbolize?)
Question 15 ◆ What Mystery was Lucia shown in the vision of 1929?

Level 4 - Lesson 12

General

Catholic Etiquette (continued)

Good manners is part of Catholic Etiquette. A child is under the authority of his parents or lawful superiors (e.g. a teacher). He must not only obey his parents and his superiors, but he must treat all adults with respect and honour.

Small things like greeting a teacher at the beginning of the day, like thanking mum for cooking dinner, and saying 'excuse me' when walking past an adult. A child should also let an adult go through the doorway before them, and should stand up and give his seat to an adult in a bus or train. If an adult enters a room, the Catholic boy or girl should stop what they are doing and stand up.

These are all little courtesies which should distinguish a Catholic child from other children.

The same could be said in the classroom at school. Children should not call out in class, they should certainly never be cheeky. A Catholic child should be a consolation to his parents and teachers, not a cross. It is actually a sin for a child to cause unnecessary grief to his parents/superiors. On the contrary, it is commendable for a child to display good manners and a sign that the child is a Catholic, not only in name, but in the way he lives his life.

Question 16 ♦ Why should a Catholic child display good manners?
Question 17 ♦ List three things a Catholic child could do at school to show his good manners.

Lesson 13

Level 4

Pre - Confirmation

Catechism

The Second Commandment of the Church

130. What is a fast day?

A fast day is a day on which only one full meal is allowed and two small collations may be taken, the quantity and quality of which are determined by approved local custom.

131. What is a day of abstinence?

A day of abstinence is a day on which we are not allowed the use of meat.

132. Who are obliged to observe the abstinence days of the Church?

All baptised persons who have reached the use of reason and passed their fourteenth birthday are obliged to observe the abstinence days of the Church, unless excused or dispensed.

As mentioned in the previous lesson, the Commandments of the Church can and do change. The Commandments on fasting and abstinence have changed in recent years and were once far stricter than what they are now. In past years, the faithful had to fast every day of Lent, now it is only commanded on Ash Wednesday and Good Friday. Of course the Church wants us to do much more than what is the bare minimum, but we must at least be aware of the Church laws in this regard.

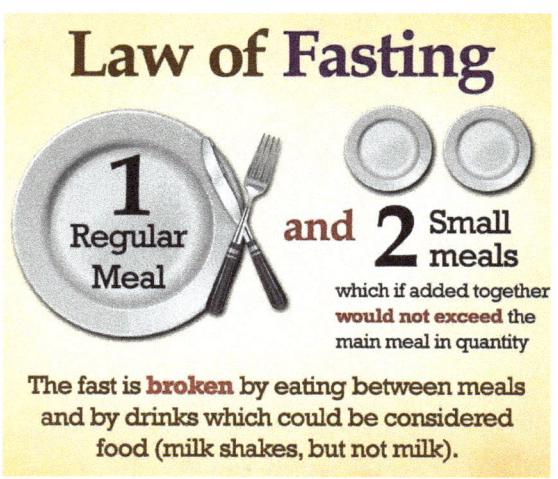

Question 1 ◆ What is a day of abstinence?
Question 2 ◆ Who are obliged to observe the abstinence days of the Church?
Question 3 ◆ What else does the Church oblige us to do on holy days of obligation?

Level 4 - Lesson 13

Prayer

The Act of Contrition (continued)

And I firmly resolve, by the help of Thy grace, never to offend Thee again

One of the conditions for our sins to be forgiven is not only that we are sorry for them, but that we resolve not to commit them again. Thus, when we pray these words, we are telling God, that with His help (grace) we will try our best not to commit these sins again. Many children and adults, when going to confession, do not think about this obligation and yet it is an essential part of our sorrow.

And carefully to avoid the occasions of sin.

Not only are we sorry for our sins and we resolve not to sin again, we must do more than that. We must avoid all occasions where we might fall into that sin. For example, if an alcoholic resolves not to drink any more, but every night walks past the hotel, and therefore often goes in and drinks, he is sinning by not avoiding (for him) this occasion of sin. Walking past a hotel would not be an occasion of sin for most people.

Amen.

So be it.

Question 4 ◆ Sorrow is not enough for a true contrition. What two other factors are necessary?

Question 5 ◆ What type of help do we need, to never offend God again?

Question 6 ◆ What is another word for contrition?

Bible Story

The Ascension

After this Jesus went with His apostles to Mount Olivet.

There He blessed them, and as He was blessing them, the wonder and power of God were shown.

Slowly, and in a bright light, Jesus was lifted from the ground, and was raised up into the skies–into heaven– as they strained their eyes to look after Him.

They were sorry to see Jesus go from them, and they remained in awe and wonder, looking up where Jesus had gone.

At last two angels in white garments spoke to the apostles, and told them: "This Jesus, whom you have seen ascending into heaven, shall come again."

The apostles praised God, and went back into Jerusalem, as our Lord had commanded, to wait for the Holy Ghost.

Question 7   ♦   What did the Apostles do after the Ascension?
Question 8   ♦   Who said to the Apostles, "This Jesus, whom you have seen ascending into heaven, shall come again."
Question 9   ♦   What power did Jesus give to His Apostles?

The Saints

Saint Cuthbert

In the valley of the Tweed, the river which divides England from Scotland, there lived a shepherd boy named Cuthbert. He was very strong and lively, spending all the time he could in games and sports, and being so good at them that he usually beat his companions in jumping and running and wrestling. Then one day something went wrong with his knee. It started to swell, and though the doctor tried to heal it, it got worse and worse. Cuthbert could no longer run about. He found it difficult even to walk. He thought he would be a cripple all his life.

But, as it turned out, he was lucky. A traveler who was passing through the valley saw him and told him of a way in which his knee might be cured. Cuthbert tried it, and he was soon quite well again – so well that he went for a short time to be a soldier in the King of Northumbria's army. But he did not ever forget the time when, because he could not lead an ordinary life like others, he was so lonely, and was asking God to make his knee better. In the end he was to become a hermit – that is, a man who lives all alone so that he can have more time to say prayers for other people. This did not happen for many years, though soon after he came home from the war he made up his mind to become a monk. One night, when he was looking after his sheep on the Grampian Hills, he suddenly saw a great light in the sky. Wondering what it could be, he looked more closely, and saw a band of angels coming down to earth and then going back into the skies carrying someone in their arms.

As the light faded he went over to his companions and asked them one by one what they thought it was. But none of them had seen it. Some of them had been asleep, and those who were awake had seen no light, and told Cuthbert that he must have been asleep and have dreamt it all. It was not till many days afterwards that Cuthbert heard the news that on that night, far away in Northumbria, Saint Aidan had died; and then he knew that, whether it was a dream or whether it was a vision, it was God's way of telling him that He wanted him to come and serve Him in the same kind of way as Saint Aidan had chosen.

So as soon as he could arrange for other people to look after the sheep for their owners he set out for the nearest monastery, which was at Melrose, and there he became a monk. Later on he was sent to Lindisfarne itself, and for twelve years was Prior there. Yet all the time he really wanted to be a hermit, and at last the Bishop let him have his wish. Not far from Lindisfarne was a tiny island – an islet – named Farne. No one lived on it, because people said that it was full of evil spirits; and there was no water there, or trees; and corn would not grow. But Cuthbert determined to make his home there, and the brethren of Lindisfarne went with him to help him build his cell. They made it of stones they found on the island, and logs of wood, and rubble and clay. It was round in shape, and the wall was so high that a person inside could see nothing but the sky above him.

Near the place where they had landed they built a house called the Hospice, where visitors could stay, for although Cuthbert was going to be a hermit he was not allowed to cut himself off altogether from the monks on Lindisfarne, who might want his advice. While they were building the Hospice they found a fine spring of water. They knew now that it would be possible to live there, if they could also grow some wheat.

The Saints

Cuthbert had brought some seeds with him, which he sowed at the right season, and he waited through the winter to see if they would come up. But when spring came there was not a stalk or a leaf to be seen. He was very disappointed, but he would try again. If wheat would not grow, he thought, perhaps barley would; so he asked the monks for some barley seed and, though it was past the proper time for sowing, he put it in at once. Almost immediately a good crop sprang up, which made him very thankful and happy. He could live there now quite alone, growing his own food, without depending on anyone, and he could spend his days in work and prayer.

In the first year he was there, however, his plans were nearly ruined by the birds. They destroyed his crop of barley, and they pecked at the other things he had sown. There were in particular two crows who started to line their nests with the straw which made the thatch of the Hospice. Other birds followed their example, and the Hospice roof practically disappeared. Cuthbert decided that this was unfair on any monks who might come over as visitors, so he solemnly sent the two crows away, telling them not to come back.

For a time no more was seen of them. Then one day, when Cuthbert was digging his field, one of them came back. With his wings drooping and his head held down, he croaked at Cuthbert, and seemed to be asking for forgiveness. Cuthbert nodded at him in a friendly way. The crow seemed to understand and quickly flew off, and came back with the other crow. They then flew round and round the Saint, cawing happily, and one of them dropped from his beak a large lump of pig's lard, which Cuthbert found very useful for greasing his boots to keep out the wet. He and the crows became friendly, and they soon learnt not to spoil his crop of barley and steal the straw on the Hospice roof.

So at last everything was alright, and Cuthbert could lead the lonely life he had so long wanted to lead. He hoped he would be able to stay on Farne till he died, but one day the King himself, with many of his nobles, and the Bishop, came over to the little island, and, when they got to Cuthbert's cell, knelt down together and begged him to come back and be made Bishop of Lindisfarne. Because Cuthbert saw that this was what God wanted him to do, he did as they asked and came back to fill the place once filled by that Saint Aidan whose soul he had seen being carried to Heaven on that night, long before, when he had been a shepherd on the hill-side.

The feast of Saint Cuthbert is March 20th.

Question 10 ◆ Whose soul did Saint Cuthbert see ascending into heaven?
Question 11 ◆ Relate the story of Saint Cuthbert and the crows.
Question 12 ◆ Against whose false teaching did Saint Germain preach?

Devotions

Devotion to the Sacred Heart of Jesus
The Nine First Fridays (continued)

The third apparition took place on 2nd July 1674, while Margaret Mary was praying before the Blessed Sacrament exposed. She saw a vision of Jesus in glory, with His five wounds shining like suns, and He then showed her His Heart on fire with love for mankind, a love that unfortunately was often ignored or treated with contempt.

He asked her to make up for this coldness and ingratitude by receiving Holy Communion as often as she was allowed, and particularly on the first Friday of each month. This idea of making reparation for the sins of others is also prominent in the messages given by Mary to the children at Fatima in 1917.

The fourth apparition, which took place on 16th of June 1675, was the most important. Again it happened as Saint Margaret Mary was praying before the Blessed Sacrament, when He again showed her a representation of His Heart, further complaining of the ingratitude and coldness of mankind towards Him, and particularly when this was the case with those specially consecrated to Him.

To make up for this He asked that the first Friday after the feast of Corpus Christi should be dedicated as a feast in honour of His Sacred Heart, when people should receive Holy Communion in reparation.

The "Great promise" associated with this devotion applied to those who went to Communion on nine consecutive First Fridays: "I promise you, in the excess of the mercy of My Heart, that Its all-powerful love will grant to all those who shall receive Communion on the first Friday of nine consecutive months the grace of final repentance; they shall not die under My displeasure nor without receiving the Sacraments, My Divine Heart becoming their assured refuge at that last hour."

These promises have been endorsed by successive Popes, and were explicitly mentioned in the bull of Saint Margaret Mary's canonization authorised by Benedict XV. This promise is really one of the grace of final repentance, that is of dying in a state of grace.

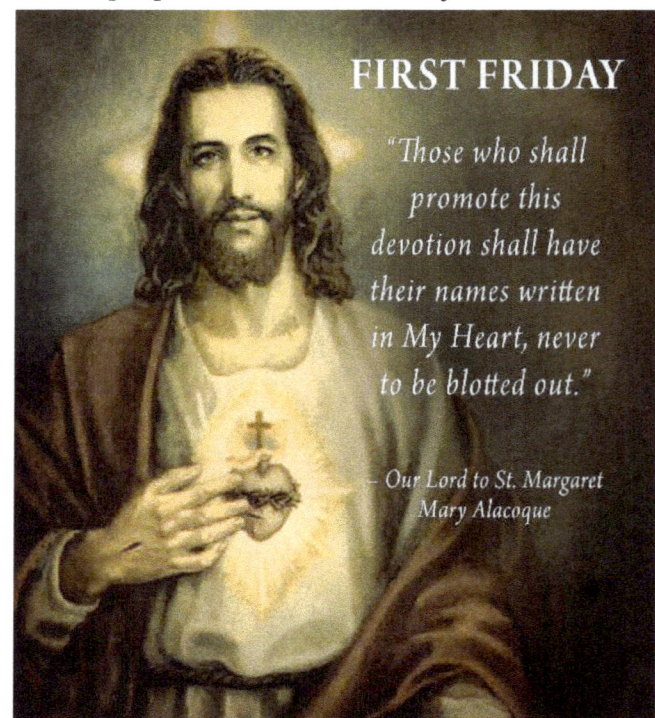

FIRST FRIDAY

"Those who shall promote this devotion shall have their names written in My Heart, never to be blotted out."

– Our Lord to St. Margaret Mary Alacoque

Question 13	◆	Of what did Our Lord complain to Saint Margaret Mary?
Question 14	◆	What is the great promise associated with the devotion of the First Fridays?
Question 15	◆	To whom did Jesus reveal the Devotion of the Nine First Fridays?

Level 4 - Lesson 13

General

Catholic Etiquette (continued)

Let us study the dress standards for the Catholic child. The most obvious standards are those of Christian modesty. These standards do not change from one year to another, or from one generation to another, or for that matter, from one century to another. What was immodest one hundred years ago, is still immodest today. God doesn't change His mind.

If general mixed bathing was immoral when your great grandparents were alive, why has it suddenly become moral in today's world? Because today's world cares little for God! It is no more moral today than it was in your great grandparents' time. Be careful of those (even Catholics) who say, "It's okay today, they went over the top in the old days". In the 1950's, Pope Pius XII said that the world was as bad then as it was in the time of Noah, when God destroyed the world. How much worse is it today? So do not be guided by the standards of today.

Another aspect of Catholic dress is fashion. Fashions in regard to dress change regularly, often for the worse (although not always). The wearing of earrings through the nose or other parts of the body are not Catholic practices and are not pleasing to God.

The selection of clothes is very important for the Catholic boy and girl. Work clothes or play clothes are good for working and playing, but they are not to be worn when attending Sunday Mass. The clothes we wear speak of the person we are. We should wear the appropriate clothes at the appropriate times. This is pleasing to God.

Question 16 ◆ Do the rules of Christian modesty change from one century to the next?
Question 17 ◆ List two fashions that are not acceptable for Catholics.
Question 18 ◆ List three things a Catholic child could do at school to show his good manners.

Lesson 14

Level 4

Pre - Confirmation

Catechism

The Third, Fourth, Fifth and Sixth Commandments of the Church

133. **What is meant by the commandment to confess our sins at least once a year?**

    By the commandment to confess our sins at least once a year is meant that we are strictly obliged to make a good confession within the year, if we have a mortal sin to confess.

134. **What sin does a Catholic commit who neglects to receive Holy Communion worthily during the Easter time?**

    A Catholic who neglects to receive Holy Communion worthily during the Easter time commits a mortal sin.

135. **What is meant by the commandment to contribute to the support of the Church?**

    By the commandment to contribute to the support of the Church is meant that each of us must help to pay the expenses of the Church.

136. **What is the ordinary law of the Church to be observed at the wedding of a Catholic?**

    The ordinary law of the Church to be observed at the wedding of a Catholic is this: A Catholic can be married only in the presence of an authorised priest and two witnesses.

The Church has many laws. The above laws complete the six chief laws (commandments) of the Church. It is important to know that the Church has the power from God to make its own laws and that these laws are binding (Catholics must obey them).

Learn by heart the six chief commandments of the Church.

Question 1 ♦ What sin does a Catholic commit who neglects to receive Holy Communion worthily during the Easter time?
Question 2 ♦ What is meant by the commandment to contribute to the support of the Church?
Question 3 ♦ What is a day of abstinence?

Level 4 - Lesson 14

Prayer

Prayer

Our work on the topic 'Prayer' has been different in this level than in previous levels. Rather than learning a new prayer each lesson, we have studied in detail what we mean when we pray these common prayers. It is very important to know and understand what we are saying in our prayers. In this lesson, we are going to revise the definition of prayer which we learnt in Level Three.

A Definition of Prayer

Prayer is the lifting up of the heart and mind to God in Adoration, Thanksgiving, Reparation and Petition. When we pray, we do not have to use words; we speak to God from our hearts; we speak to the one we love. We praise God, we thank Him, we make reparation for our own sins and for the sins of others and we ask for God's help.

Question 4 ◆ Write out the definition of prayer
Question 5 ◆ For what do we make reparation?
Question 6 ◆ Sorrow is not enough for a true contrition. What two other factors are necessary?

Bible Story

The Coming of the Holy Ghost

For nine days after the Ascension of Jesus into Heaven, the apostles and other friends of Jesus and His Mother Mary prayed together in Jerusalem, waiting for the coming of the Holy Ghost.

On the tenth day, suddenly there was a sound like the rushing of wind, and what looked like tongues of fire came and rested on the head of every one of them. They were all filled with the Holy Ghost, and they were able to speak languages that they had never learnt. This was the first Pentecost Sunday.

Then Saint Peter preached to a great crowd. He told them that Jesus had risen from the dead, that the Holy Ghost had come down, and that they ought to be baptised. About 3,000 people believed, and were baptised that day.

Question 7 ◆ What is the name of the day that we commemorate the coming of the Holy Ghost?
Question 8 ◆ How many people were baptised on the very first Pentecost Sunday?
Question 9 ◆ What happened on the first Pentecost Sunday?

The Saints

Saint Wenceslaus

Good King Wenceslas is a Christmas Carol that tells the story of a king's journey through harsh winter weather. His intention is to bring food and firewood to a poor man he notices from the tower of his castle during the Feast of Stephen on December 26. The Christmas Carol is based on the real King, 'Saint Wenceslaus'. That was how men thought of him at the time, just as they thought of his twin brother as 'bad King Boleslaus.'

The story really begins with his grandmother, Ludmilla, who brought him up and who also was a saint. She was the wife of a Duke of Bohemia, in the south of Germany, and she and her husband were both converted to Christianity about a hundred years after Saint Boniface died. Some say they were converted by monks from England, who were carrying on Saint Boniface's work. Ludmilla brought up her son as a Christian, and in time, on his father's death, he became Duke of Bohemia and married a princess named Drahomira, who pretended to be a Christian but secretly was still a pagan and wanted to turn all Bohemia pagan again. They had twin children, Wenceslaus and Boleslaus, who were eight years old when their father died in 918 A.D. Wenceslaus who, as the elder, now became Duke, was sent just before his father's death to be brought up by his grandmother, Saint Ludmilla; while Boleslaus remained with his mother, Drahomira, who made him a pagan like herself.

As the boys grew up it became quite clear that there would be a clash between them. Drahomira was supported by the pagan party, but the people so loved Ludmilla, who was the protectress of the Christians, that Drahomira was unable to do anything against her. And more and more people began to see that Wenceslaus was turning into a mild, merciful, and just young man who would be an admirable ruler, while Boleslaus was fierce, cruel, and treacherous, and entirely under his mother's influence.

At last Drahomira decided to have Ludmilla murdered. She found two of her courtiers, who were great worshipers of the pagan gods and looked on the Christians with hatred, to undertake it. They went to Ludmilla's palace, where they found her kneeling at her prayers before a cross in her private chapel. They crept up behind her and strangled her with her own veil.

Wenceslaus, when his grandmother was dead – though he did not know then that it was his mother who had her murdered – realised that the pagan forces were too strong for him to face alone. He put Bohemia under the direct protection of the Emperor, who gave him the title of King, and provided him with monks and priests from the Christians in Bohemia. He also granted Wenceslaus the right to carry on his shield and standard the black Imperial eagle when he found at last that he had to fight to save the Faith in his land.

In the battle which he fought against the pagans, King Wenceslaus was victorious, and some men said that they saw two angels guarding him through the fiercest of the conflict. But before it was over the angels had left him, and the superstitious feared that the King was killed. Wenceslaus, however, was still alive, though he was in deadly danger. After the battle his mother, Drahomira, asked him to come and visit her to talk matters over. The King, even though by now he knew her wickedness,

Level 4 - Lesson 14

The Saints

was still an obedient son and went at her bidding to Bunzlau, where she was. As he entered the town he went first to the church there to pray, but at the church door he was murdered by his brother, Boleslaus,

Three years after the murder Boleslaus repented of his awful deed, and had Wenceslaus reburied in the great church at Prague, the capital of Bohemia, and himself renounced his paganism. By his death, indeed, Wenceslaus did what in his lifetime he had never been able to do – made Bohemia Christian. And within thirty years of his martyrdom the Faith was so strong that Wenceslaus's friend, the Emperor Otto, gave Bohemia a bishop of its own with his seat in the Cathedral of Prague, where the good King lay in a shrine to which pilgrims came from all over Germany.

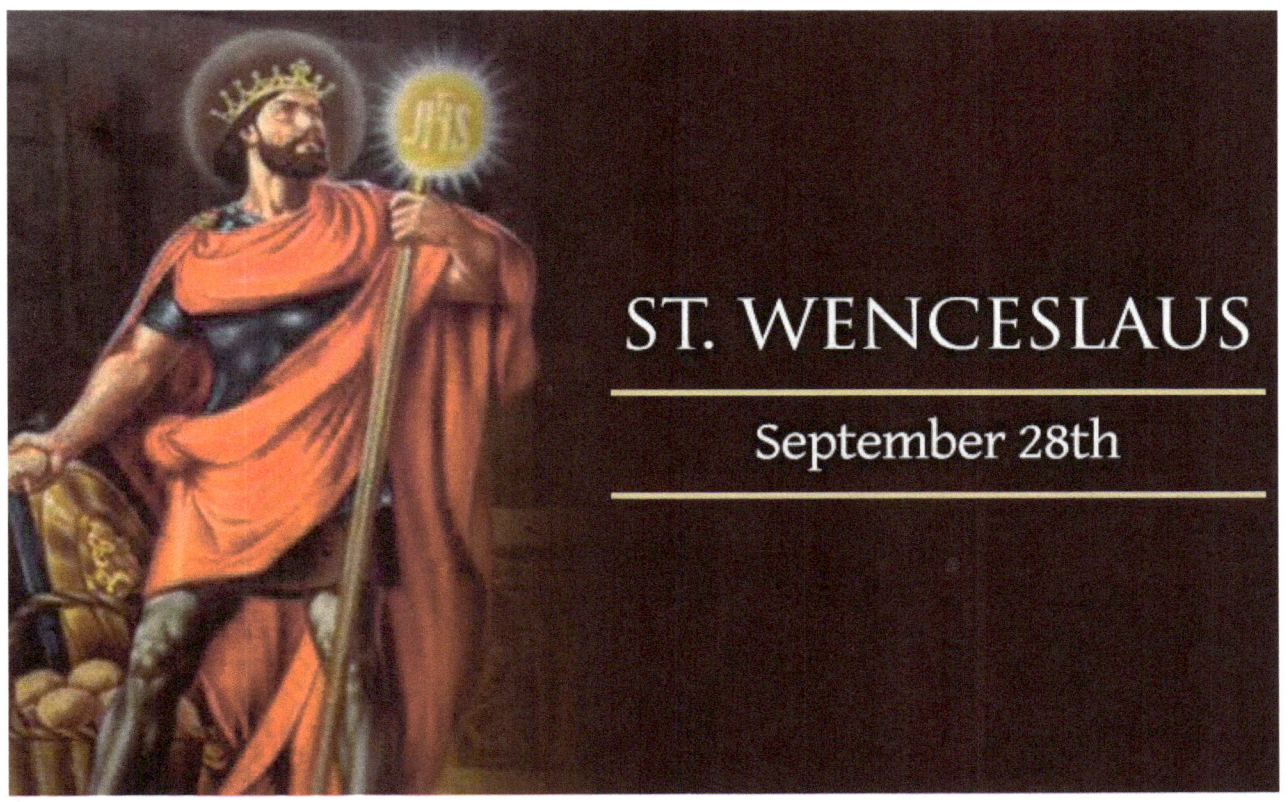

Question 10 ◆ Who was the grandmother of Saint Wenceslaus?
Question 11 ◆ What was Saint Wenceslaus able to do by his death which he could not do in his life?
Question 12 ◆ Whose soul did Saint Cuthbert see ascending into heaven?

Devotions

Devotion to the Sacred Heart of Jesus
The Nine First Fridays (continued)

Listed below are the promises made to Saint Margaret Mary

"I promise you, in the excessive mercy of My Heart that My all-powerful love will grant to all those who receive Holy Communion on the First Friday for nine consecutive months, the grace of final repentance; they shall not die in My disgrace nor without receiving the sacraments; My Divine Heart shall be their safe refuge in that last moment."

1) I will give them all the graces necessary for their state in life.

2) I will give peace in their families.

3) I will console them in all their troubles.

4) They shall find in My Heart an assured refuge during life and especially at the hour of death.

5) I will pour abundant blessings on all their undertakings.

6) Sinners shall find in My Heart the source and infinite ocean of mercy.

7) Tepid souls shall become fervent.

8) Fervent souls shall speedily rise to great perfection.

9) I will bless the homes in which the image of My Sacred Heart shall be exposed and honoured.

10) I will give to priests the power to touch the most hardened hearts.

11) Those who propagate this devotion shall have their name written in My Heart, and it shall never be effaced.

12) The all-powerful love of My Heart will grant to all those who shall receive Communion on the First Friday of nine consecutive months the grace of final repentance; they shall not die under My displeasure, nor without receiving their Sacraments; My Heart shall be their assured refuge at the last hour.

Question 13 ♦ How many promises did Our Lord make to Saint Margaret Mary?
Question 14 ♦ What is the main promise made to those who make the nine First Fridays?
Question 15 ♦ What did Our Lord complain of to Saint Margaret Mary?

Level 4 - Lesson 14

General

Catholic Etiquette (continued)

Over the past few lessons we have studied various points in how to live our day to day lives as Catholics. It is sometimes difficult to remember all the rules and suggestions that are presented even in these lessons. But there is one rule we should never forget, one rule that should be the guiding light of our lives; **in all things we do, do them for Jesus.**
If we do this, we will be living as good, Catholic children and we will be pleasing to God.

Question 16	◆	What is the most important thing we can do as Catholic children?
Question 17	◆	Do the rules of Christian modesty change from one century to the next?
Question 18	◆	Why should a Catholic child display good manners?

Lesson 15

Level 4

Pre - Confirmation

Catechism

This is the last lesson of the year and is different to all other lessons, as there are no new questions, nor is there any new work to learn, nor is there a test to complete. It is a summary of all you have learned this year.

There are two reasons why such a summary of your work is important. Firstly, it gives you the opportunity to review all the things you have already studied, so that you have a better knowledge of your work and you will therefore be more pleasing to God. Secondly, it will serve as a good preparation for your confirmation.

88. What is the first commandment of God?
The first commandment of God is: I am the Lord thy God; thou shalt not have strange gods before Me.

89. What are we commanded by the first commandment?
By the first commandment we are commanded to offer to God alone the supreme worship that is due Him.

90. How do we worship God?
We worship God by acts of faith, hope, and charity, and by adoring Him and praying to Him.

91. How does a Catholic sin against faith?
A Catholic sins against faith by not believing what God has revealed, and by taking part in non-Catholic worship.

92. What are the sins against hope?
The sins against hope are presumption and despair.

93. What are the chief sins against charity?
The chief sins against charity are hatred of God and of our neighbour, envy, sloth, and scandal.

94. Does the first commandment forbid us to honour the saints in heaven?
The first commandment does not forbid us to honour the saints in heaven, as long as we do not give them the honour that belongs to God alone.

95. When we pray to the saints what do we ask them to do?
When we pray to the saints we ask them to offer their prayers to God for us.

Catechism

96. Do we pray to the crucifix or to the images of Christ and of the saints?
We do not pray to the crucifix or to the images of Christ and of the saints, but to the persons of whom they remind us

97. What is the second commandment of God?
The second commandment of God is: Thou shalt not take the name of the Lord thy God in vain.

98. What are we commanded by the second commandment?
By the second commandment we are commanded always to speak with reverence of God, of the saints, and of holy things.

99. What is meant by taking God's name in vain?
By taking God's name in vain is meant that the name of God or the holy name of Jesus Christ is used without reverence.

100. What is cursing?
Cursing is the calling down of some evil on a person, place, or thing.

101. What is the third commandment of God?
The third commandment of God is: Remember thou keep holy the Lord's day.

102. What are we commanded by the third commandment?
By the third commandment we are commanded to worship God in a special manner on Sunday, the Lord's day.

103. How does the Church command us to worship God on Sunday?
The Church commands us to worship God on Sunday by assisting at the Holy Sacrifice of the Mass.

104. What is forbidden by the third commandment of God?
By the third commandment of God all unnecessary servile work on Sunday is forbidden.

105. What is servile work?
Servile work is that which requires labour of body rather than of mind.

106. What is the fourth commandment of God?
The fourth commandment of God is: Honour thy father and thy mother.

Catechism

107. What are we commanded by the fourth commandment?
By the fourth commandment we are commanded to respect and love our parents, to obey them in all that is not sinful, and to help them when they are in need.

108. What does the fourth commandment forbid?
The fourth commandment forbids disrespect, unkindness, and disobedience to our parents and lawful superiors.

109. What is the fifth commandment of God?
The fifth commandment of God is: Thou shalt not kill.

110. What are we commanded by the fifth commandment?
By the fifth commandment we are commanded to take proper care of our own spiritual and bodily well-being and that of our neighbour.

111. What does the fifth commandment forbid?
The fifth commandment forbids murder and suicide, and also fighting, anger, hatred, revenge, drunkenness, reckless driving, and bad example.

112. What is the sixth commandment?
The sixth commandment of God is: Thou shalt not commit adultery.

113. What are we commanded by the sixth commandment?
By the sixth commandment we are commanded to be pure and modest in our behaviour.

114. What does the sixth commandment forbid?
The sixth commandment forbids all impurity and immodesty in words, looks, and actions, whether alone or with others.

115. What is the seventh commandment?
The seventh commandment of God is: Thou shalt not steal.

116. What are we commanded by the seventh commandment?
By the seventh commandment we are commanded to respect what belongs to others.

117. What does the seventh commandment forbid?
The seventh commandment forbids all dishonesty, such as stealing, cheating, unjust keeping of what belongs to others, and unjust damage to the property of others.

Catechism

118. Are we obliged to restore to the owner stolen goods, or their value?
We are obliged to restore to the owner stolen goods, or their value, whenever we are able.

119. What is the eighth commandment of God?
The eighth commandment of God is: Thou shalt not bear false witness against thy neighbour.

120. What are we commanded by the eighth commandment?
By the eighth commandment we are commanded to speak the truth in all things.

121. What does the eighth commandment forbid?
The eighth commandment forbids lies and harming the name of another.

122. What is the ninth commandment of God?
The ninth commandment of God is: Thou shalt not covet thy neighbour's wife.

123. What are we commanded by the ninth commandment?
By the ninth commandment we are commanded to be pure in thought and in desire.

124. What is forbidden by the ninth commandment?
The ninth commandment forbids all thoughts and desires contrary to chastity.

125. What is the tenth commandment of God?
The tenth commandment of God is: Thou shalt not covet thy neighbours goods.

126. What does the tenth commandment forbid?
The tenth commandment forbids all desire to take or to keep unjustly what belongs to others, and also forbids envy at their success.

127. Which are the chief commandments, or laws, of the Church?
The chief commandments, or laws, of the Church are these six:
  1) *To assist at Mass on all Sundays and holy days of obligation.*
  2) *To fast and to abstain on the days appointed.*
  3) *To confess our sins at least once a year.*
  4) *To receive Holy Communion during the Easter time.*
  5) *To contribute to the support of the Church.*
  6) *To observe the laws of the Church concerning marriage.*

Catechism

128. What sin does a Catholic commit who through his own fault misses Mass on a Sunday or holy day of obligation?
A Catholic who through his own fault misses Mass on a Sunday or holy day of obligation commits a mortal sin.

129. What else does the Church oblige us to do on holy days of obligation?
The Church obliges us to abstain from servile work on holy days of obligation, just as on Sundays, as far as we are able.

130. What is a fast day?
A fast day is a day on which only one full meal is allowed and two small collations may be taken, the quantity and quality of which are determined by approved local custom.

131. What is a day of abstinence?
A day of abstinence is a day on which we are not allowed the use of meat.

132. Who are obliged to observe the abstinence days of the Church?
All baptised persons who have reached the use of reason and passed their fourteenth birthday are obliged to observe the abstinence days of the Church, unless excused or dispensed.

133. What is meant by the commandment to confess our sins at least once a year?
By the commandment to confess our sins at least once a year is meant that we are strictly obliged to make a good confession within the year, if we have a mortal sin to confess.

134. What sin does a Catholic commit who neglects to receive Holy Communion worthily during the Easter time?
A Catholic who neglects to receive Holy Communion worthily during the Easter time commits a mortal sin.

135. What is meant by the commandment to contribute to the support of the Church?
By the commandment to contribute to the support of the Church is meant that each of us must help to pay the expenses of the Church.

Level 4 - Lesson 15

Catechism

136. **What is the ordinary law of the Church to be observed at the wedding of a Catholic?**

    The ordinary law of the Church to be observed at the wedding of a Catholic is this: A Catholic can be married only in the presence of an authorised priest and two witnesses.